# The Symphony ∼1720–1840

## Series B ∼ Volume IX

Friedrich Witt ∼ One Symphony

Antoine Reicha ∼ Two Symphonies

Anton Eberl ∼ One Symphony

# The Symphony
## 1720-1840

A comprehensive collection of full scores
in sixty volumes

# Barry S. Brook

EDITOR–IN–CHIEF

## Barbara B. Heyman
ASSOCIATE EDITOR

# A Garland Series

# Contents of Collection

# Series B ∿ Volume IX

## Friedrich Witt *(1770–1836)*

### One Symphony

Them. Index 2

Edited by
Stephen C. Fisher

## Antoine Reicha *(1770–1836)*

### Two Symphonies

Edited by
Stephen C. Fisher

## Anton Eberl *(1765–1807)*

### One Symphony

Op. 33

Edited by
Barbara Coeyman and Stephen C. Fisher

*Garland Publishing, Inc.*
*New York & London   1983*

Library of Congress Cataloging in Publication Data

Witt, Friedrich, 1770–1836.
    [Symphonies, no. 2, D major]
    One symphony, them. index 2.

    (The Symphony, 1720–1840. Series B ; Volume IX)
    Includes bibliographies.
    Includes thematic indexes for Witt and Eberl.
    Contents: Symphony no. 2 in D major / Friedrich
Witt—Symphonie à petit orchestre no. 1 in C minor ;
Symphony no. 3 in F major / Antoine Reicha—Symphony in
E-flat major, op. 33 / Anton Eberl.
    1. Symphonies—Scores.  I. Reicha, Antoine,
1770–1836.  II. Eberl, Anton, 1765–1807. Symphonies, op.
33, E♭ major. 1983.  III. Series.
M1001.W835 no. 2  1983    83-14244
ISBN 0-8240-3838-X

The volumes in this series have been printed on acid-free,
250-year-life paper.

Printed in the United States of America

# Contents

*Thematic Index number

# Illustrations

# Introduction

## Beethoven and the three composers in this volume

For posterity . . . no symphonies are more obscure than those of Beethoven's contemporaries, Schubert alone excepted. Once Beethoven's masterpieces were appreciated they effectively eliminated all competitors.[1]

With this epitaph, Nicholas Temperley sums up the fate of a generation of symphonists, including the three composers represented in this volume. In 1836, when Friedrich Witt and Antoine Reicha died, their symphonies, as well as those of the long-deceased Anton Eberl, had been largely forgotten. Tastes had changed, and even the once-popular Witt had gone out of fashion. Until very recently twentieth-century scholarship has taken little notice of the symphonies of these three composers, aside from the "Jena" symphony of Witt, which was studied mainly with a view to deciding its authenticity. Research on the symphony as a whole has been primarily directed at the issues of the origin and early development of the form. Furthermore, the nineteenth century is still at an early stage of investigation; paradoxically, it seems a familiar period but at the same time contains much unexplored territory.

The above generalities apply in good measure to all three composers under discussion. Eberl, the oldest, is under the most satisfactory bibliographical control, with a recent thematic catalogue[2] and a substantial listing of editions in *RISM*, Series

[1] Nicholas Temperley, "Symphony, II. 19th century," *The new Grove dictionary of music and musicians*, ed. Stanley Sadie, 20 vols. (London: Macmillan, 1980) XVIII, 454.
  One of the objectives of *The Symphony 1720–1840* is to publish representative scores by Beethoven's leading "competitors" and contemporaries throughout Europe and the Americas: *The northern Italian symphony, 1800–1840* (A/VI), Gänsbacher, Danzi (C/V), Ries (C/XII), Kalliwoda, Herold and Onslow (D/IX), Méhul (D/VIII), Rebeyrol (D/VII), Sterndale Bennett (E/VII), Haigh, Potter, S. S. Wesley (E/III), Smethergell (E/III), Falbe (F/I), del Moral (F/IV), de Mayo (F/IV), Nonó (F/IV), Dobrzyński (F/VII), Berwald (F/III), Bomtempo (F/V), Eggert (F/III), Hartmann (F/VI), Heinrich, Nuñes Garcia, and Weyse (F/VI). B.S.B.

[2] In A. Duane White, "The piano works of Anton Eberl (1765–1807)" (Ph.D. diss., University of Wisconsin, 1971); this supersedes one in Franz Joseph Ewens, *Anton Eberl: Ein Beitrag zur Musikgeschichte in Wien um 1800* (Dresden: Limpert, 1927).

A/I. For Reicha we have a useful if not wholly satisfactory catalogue;[3] research on Witt is in such a primitive state that the Thematic Index of his symphonies in this volume represents the first published attempt to inventory any aspect of his work in detail. Before 1960, two symphonies by these three men had been published in modern editions, both incorrectly attributed: an Eberl symphony as a work of Mozart and a Witt symphony as a work of Beethoven, both juvenile productions. Since then two further juvenile works of Witt and two Reicha symphonies have appeared in print, but the present volume represents the first publication in score of a mature symphony by either Witt or Eberl.

Although the three composers do not constitute a school in any meaningful sense, they do have links to each other and to Beethoven that make it worthwhile to consider them as a group. Witt's connections to the others are relatively tenuous. He may have encountered Reicha at Wallerstein in the early 1780's. Witt met Haydn (who figures in the biographies of all these younger composers) at Wallerstein in December 1790 and again in Vienna in July 1796; conceivably Beethoven was around on the latter occasion. From then on, though, Witt is active in different places than the others. Reicha, Eberl, and Beethoven were much more closely associated with each other. From Reicha's arrival in Bonn in 1785 to Beethoven's departure in 1792 the two young men seem to have been close friends. They would have met Haydn in December 1790 and seen him on many occasions thereafter. Beethoven and Eberl must have seen quite a bit of each other in Vienna in the early 1790's in the former Mozart circle. After 1801 Reicha was in Vienna and Eberl had returned from his Russian sojourns; they and

Beethoven were moving in the same spheres, particularly the one around Prince Lobkowitz. Eberl's death in 1807 and Reicha's departure for Paris in 1808 ended the contact among the three.

Considering symphonic production specifically, Eberl, Reicha, and Witt all began composing symphonies while in their teens; Beethoven, who at sixteen had played viola in Reicha's first symphony, waited until the age of twenty-nine to compose his own. On the other hand, Beethoven seems to have got his first symphony into print ahead of the three slightly older composers represented in this volume: his Op. 21, first performed on 2 April 1800, was published by Hoffmeister & Kühnel in Leipzig about the end of 1801. Reicha's Opp. 41 and 42 were probably issued by Breitkopf & Härtel in 1803, and Witt's first two to be published appeared from André about the end of that year. Meanwhile, Beethoven had composed his Op. 36 in 1802 and performed it for the first time in his concert on 5 April 1803, with Eberl in the audience.[4] By this time, Eberl would have been about finished with Op. 33, which presumably received its first performances about the middle of 1803 at one of the residences of its dedicatee, Prince Lobkowitz. The first public performance of this work came on 6 January 1804. Lobkowitz had already taken an interest in the new symphony Beethoven had under way; a letter of 22 October 1803 from Ferdinand Ries to the publisher Simrock indicates that Beethoven was impressing his circle with performances of this third symphony on the piano and that the prince had offered the phenomenal sum of 400 ducats for the dedication and six months' exclusive rights to the work.[5] The "Eroica" must first have been performed toward the middle of 1804; Lobkowitz was showing it off to Prince Louis Ferdinand of Prussia at his country

---

[3] In Olga Šotolová, *Antonín Rejcha* (Prague: Supraphon, 1977); this catalogue contains only minimal information about each work and lacks a numbering system, so that references to it must be made by page rather than work number.

[4] See n. 93 below.

[5] Quoted in Georg Kinsky and Hans Halm, *Das Werk Beethovens* (Munich: Henle, 1955) 131.

seat that summer.[6] As will be seen later, Eberl must have encountered the "Eroica" in this period, for he paid homage to it in his next symphony, Op. 34, which he performed on 25 January 1805. By this time the "Eroica" had received a semi-public performance at Lobkowitz's palace and another (on 13 or 20 January 1805)[7] at the home of the banker von Würth; the first public performance came on 7 April 1805.

By the end of 1806, Beethoven's Opp. 36 and 55 had appeared in print from the Viennese Bureau des arts et d'industrie, while Eberl had published his Op. 33 with Kühnel and Op. 34 with Breitkopf & Härtel and Witt had brought out his Nos. 3 and 4 with André. This brought the total of symphonies published by the four composers to eleven in five years—curiously, five of them (Reicha's Opp. 41 and 42, Eberl's Op. 33, Beethoven's Op. 55, and Witt's No. 4) in E-flat major! As late as this it was not altogether clear which of the four composers was going to be the dominant figure of the group. The matter was to resolve itself fairly quickly thereafter, however, as the "Eroica" gained repeated hearings. Eberl was not to compose another symphony, and Reicha, who continued to write symphonies, did not see another one in print. Only Witt was to enjoy any great degree of success as a symphonist in the next years.

Eberl died in March 1807, ironically in the same month as a semi-public performance of Beethoven's Symphony No. 4, Op. 60 (possibly it had been performed privately a bit earlier at the residence of the dedicatee, Count Oppersdorff, in

Silesia).[8] The year 1808 was a busy one for all the living composers of the group: Witt published his Symphonies No. 5 and 6 and Beethoven and Reicha each finished several new works. Beethoven's Opp. 67 and 68 were completed in the first months of the year. Apparently Lobkowitz and Count Rasumovsky purchased the dedications and six months' exclusive rights to the works as of 1 June; the first performances of the new symphonies probably came early in that month.[9] Public performances of both came on 22 December. Reicha, whose symphonic oeuvre is difficult to trace chronologically, seems to have engaged in a burst of productivity late in the year that can be documented by dated autograph scores. A Symphony No. 1 in G major is dated 13 July and a No. 3 in F major is dated 4 September; No. 2 of this group cannot presently be identified. Conceivably Reicha knew the new Beethoven works while he was composing his 1808 symphonies, but this is certainly not discernible in the music; Reicha and Beethoven seem to have gone in very different directions artistically in their mature years. Reicha left Vienna for good later in the fall; it is not known if any of the new symphonies were performed in Vienna, and by Reicha's own account No. 3 waited until 7 May 1809 in Paris for its

---

[6]Alexander W. Thayer, *Ludwig van Beethovens Leben*, ed. and trans. Hermann Deiters and Hugo Riemann, 5 vols. (Leipzig: Breitkopf & Härtel, 1907–1923; reprint, Hildesheim: Olms, 1970–1972; hereafter called *TDR*) II, 426–28; also published as *The life of Ludwig van Beethoven*, ed. Henry Krebiehl, 3 vols. (New York: The Beethoven Association, 1921; hereafter called *TK*) II, 26; also *Thayer's life of Beethoven*, ed. Elliot Forbes, 2 vols. (Princeton: Princeton University Press, 1967; hereafter called *TF*), 350–51; *TF* unaccountably omits the date of the incident.

[7]See n. 82 below.

[8]On the March performances, see *TDR* III, 8–9; *TK* II, 100–02; *TF* I, 416–17. Oppersdorff paid Beethoven 500 florins for Op. 60 on 2 February 1807; see *TDR* III, 9–12; *TK* II, 122–23; *TF* I, 431–32.

[9]On 8 June 1808 Beethoven told Breitkopf & Härtel that the two symphonies could not be published for six months after 1 June; *The letters of Beethoven*, ed. and trans. Emily Anderson, 3 vols. (New York: St. Martin's, 1961), No. 167; *Ludwig van Beethovens sämtliche Briefe*, ed. Emerich Kastner and Julius Kapp (Leipzig, 1923; reprint, Tutzing: Schneider, 1975; hereafter called *KK*), No. 156. On 1 November 1808 Beethoven told Oppersdorff that he had been forced to sell the symphonies to someone else (Anderson, 178; *KK*, 170). As the published editions are dedicated to Lobkowitz and Rasumovsky, there seems little reason to doubt that they had followed the usual practice of buying the rights for six months. Peter Gülke, *Zur Neuausgabe der Sinfonie Nr. 5 von Ludwig van Beethoven* (New York: Peters, 1978) 76–77, maintains that a set of parts to the work in the former Lobkowitz collection, **CS** Pnm X. G. c. 16, constitutes the original performance material.

first performance. Whether Reicha wrote more symphonies in Paris cannot be established due to the bibliographical confusion surrounding much of his oeuvre. Witt published his Symphonies No. 7 and 8 in 1810/1811, but added only one more to his total some five years later. Beethoven, of course, composed Opp. 92 and 93 in 1812 and completed his one remaining symphony in 1823. Thus nearly the entire mature symphonic output of all four composers falls within a little over a decade.

Witt, Reicha, and Eberl could all to a large extent hold their own with Beethoven's earlier works. It was only with the "Eroica" that Beethoven proved himself unmistakably to be a symphonist of greater stature than the rest of his generation. In evaluating these other composers, it must be taken into account that they were not necessarily trying to do the same things. Witt is a conservative, except occasionally in orchestration; his symphonies by and large stay within the stylistic limits established by the previous generation. Eberl and Reicha are avant-garde figures, confronting a wide range of stylistic issues involving harmony, rhythm, orchestration, and form. Reicha's symphonies stay outwardly in the standard mold, but the contents include many new elements: harmonic twists, unusual cadential formulas, and rhythmic surprises. Reicha may have had trouble integrating these new elements with the older ones in his style, but his music is almost always worth listening to; he may well be the best composer of the three. Finally, Eberl, the oldest of the trio, is the most determinedly radical. He exhibits the greatest stylistic affinity with Beethoven, even extending to issues of large-scale harmonic and formal design where it might be thought Beethoven stood completely alone. While Eberl's reach definitely exceeded his grasp, at least some of his works can still hold their own and his historical importance deserves greater recognition.

# Friedrich Witt

## Life and works

Although our biographical knowledge of Friedrich Witt is far from satisfactory, it is generally accepted that he was born in Niederstetten on 8 November 1770 and that his father was Johann Caspar Witt, cantor in the Hohenlohe establishment at Weikersheim.[10] Presumably he received his earliest musical instruction from his father. Gerber states that Witt was a composition pupil of Antonio Rosetti;[11] this has never been documented, but in view of Witt's later activity at the Oettingen-Wallerstein court it certainly seems possible. To have studied with Rosetti, Witt must have been at Wallerstein for some time before Rosetti's departure in early 1789; conceivably he encountered the Reichas before they left in 1785. Be that as it may, in January 1790 Witt formally joined the Wallerstein Kapelle as a cellist.[12] As four copies of Witt symphonies made in 1790 still survive in the Wallerstein collection, it is clear that Witt was composing symphonies as early as

[10] Ludwig Schiedermair, "Die Blütezeit der Öttingen-Wallerstein'schen Hofkapelle," *Sammelbände der internationalen Musikgesellschaft* IX (1907/1980) 100, n. 2, lists two children named Friedrich born to J. C. Witt, the other born on 15 January 1773; the older son is presumed to be the composer.

[11] Ernst Ludwig Gerber, *Neues historisch-biographisches Lexikon der Tonkünstler*, 4 vols. (Leipzig: Kühnel, 1812–1814) IV, cols. 593–94.

[12] Schiedermair, "Öttingen-Wallerstein," 100. For a recent survey of musical activity at Wallerstein, see Sterling E. Murray, ed., *Seven symphonies from the court of Oettingen-Wallerstein*, in The Symphony 1720–1840, Series C, VI, Barry S. Brook, editor-in-chief (New York: Garland, 1981).

the age of nineteen. In December 1790 Witt would have met Haydn when the older composer visited Wallerstein on his way to London. Haydn sent copies of at least four of the symphonies from the first London visit to Wallerstein on his return to Vienna in 1792;[13] the impact these works had on Witt can readily be heard in the "Jena" symphony (Them. Index 14).

By the mid-1790's Witt was becoming known well beyond the confines of the Wallerstein court. In 1794 he and the clarinettist Joseph Beer went on tour as far as Potsdam, where Witt's symphonies were well received.[14] In July 1796 they were in Vienna, where Witt reported:

> Every Saturday morning at seven there is a con-cert in the Augarten; the day before yesterday I brought out a symphony and Bär [Beer] played a concerto of mine; presumably the director must have trumpeted the news around, for Wranizci [Wranitzky], Girowez [Gyrowetz], and our Fa-ther Haydn were there. . . .[15]

(Possibly Beethoven was also on hand; he presum-ably returned from his trip to Berlin during this month.[16])

Witt seems to have severed his connection with the Wallerstein court about this time and become peripatetic for a few years. His cantata *Die Auferstehung Jesu*, composed for the Prussian court, was a decided success. Another choral work, *Die vier Menschenalter*, was performed in Würzburg in 1801 to commemorate the end of the eighteenth century, and a Singspiel, *Palma*, was given in Frankfurt in the same year. The premiere of Witt's oratorio *Der leidende Heiland* in Würzburg

in 1802 led to his being offered the post of Kapell-meister to the episcopal court there.[17]

Witt resided in Würzburg for the rest of his life. In 1803 the city was secularized and for a number of years Witt was Kapellmeister to the Grand Duke of Würzburg. He also took over the direction of the city's civic orchestra, the *Harmoniekonzerte* or *Winterkonzerte*. Witt's cham-ber and orchestral music appeared in numerous editions from such publishers as André, Schott, and Breitkopf & Härtel. A comic opera, *Das Fischerweib*, was performed in Würzburg in 1807. In the course of the second decade of the century, however, Witt's star began to dim. In 1814 Würzburg was incorporated into Bavaria, and Witt's Kapelle was disbanded. Witt became Kapellmeister at the Würzburg theater; incidental music for the tragedy *Leander und Blandine* dates from this year. His last symphony to be published appeared about 1816, and in 1818 he gave up the direction of the *Winterkonzerte*. He retained his position as Kapellmeister at the theater until his death, but there is little indication of composi-tional activity in his last twenty years. From Janu-ary 1833 to January 1834 Witt's subordinates at the Würzburg theater included a young chorus master named Richard Wagner, who was composing *Die Feen* at the time. Witt died on 3 January 1836; he was remembered at the time chiefly as a composer of sacred music.[18]

A comprehensive inventory of Witt's works has not yet been attempted. It appears that the Witt material in Würzburg itself was destroyed by fire;[19] the loss of this collection has deprived Witt research of the type of focal point that the Paris

---

[13] The MSS are still in the Wallerstein collection; see Gertraut Haberkamp, compiler, *Thematischer Katalog der Musik-handschriften der Fürstlich Oettingen-Wallerstein'schen Bibliothek Schloss Harburg* (Munich: Henle, 1976) 100–01; also H. C. Robbins Landon, *Haydn: chronicle and works*, 5 vols. (Bloom-ington: Indiana University Press, 1976–1980) III, 507–08.

[14] Schiedermair, "Öttingen-Wallerstein," 100.

[15] Quoted in Schiedermair, "Öttingen-Wallerstein," 100, n. 4; all translations in this volume are mine.

[16] *TDR* II, 18; *TK* I, 198; *TF* I, 187.

[17] According to Gerber. On musical life in Würzburg in this period, see Oskar Kaul, *Musica herbipolensis: Aus Würzburgs musikalischer Vergangenheit*, ed. Frohmut Dangel-Hofmann (Marktbreit: Siegfried Gress, 1980).

[18] See *Allgemeine musikalische Zeitung* (hereafter called AMZ) XXXIX (1837) cols. 347–48.

[19] Fritz Zobeley, "Vorbemerkung," *Friedrich Witt: Symphonie B-dur* (Them. Index 12) (Wiesbaden: Breitkopf & Härtel, 1968). Hermann Beck, "Alte Musikbestände der Hofkirche zu Würzburg," *Die Musikforschung* XVII (1964) 45–51, lists no Witt MSS in that collection.

Conservatoire collection has provided investigation of the works of Reicha. Besides the choral and theatrical works listed above, Witt wrote a great deal of church music, including a number of

Masses. His instrumental works included over twenty symphonies, perhaps a like number of concertos, and a large quantity of chamber music for diverse ensembles.

## The affair of the "Jena" symphony (Them. Index 14)

In 1911, the German scholar Fritz Stein announced a remarkable discovery: a set of parts in the library of the University of Jena to an otherwise unknown C major symphony bearing an ascription (on the violin II and cello parts) to Ludwig van Beethoven. The provenance of the manuscript could not be established (Stein reported that the paper matched that of a copy of the Witt Symphony in A major, Them. Index 16), but the letters "P.F.W." in a corner of the violin I suggested that the manuscript might have been the property of Beethoven's friend Franz Wegeler. From the resemblance of certain passages to corresponding spots in the Haydn symphonies of 1791–1792, notably Nos. 93 and 97, Stein concluded that the work could have been composed no earlier than 1792. Numerous "Beethovenian" passages persuaded Stein to accept the attribution on the manuscript: this was a lost Beethoven symphony.[20]

Not everyone thought the work genuine. The Kinsky-Halm Beethoven catalogue listed the work as Anhang 1, indicating considerable doubt on the matter; they cited a comment by Hermann Kretzschmar that the piece would probably turn out to be by someone like Vaňhal, Pleyel, or Rosetti.[21] Robert Simpson, after making some perceptive observations on the relationship of the first two movements of the symphony to Haydn's No. 97, proposed that only the last movement (probably the best of the four) was by

Beethoven.[22] It was nearly half a century after Stein's original discovery that H. C. Robbins Landon announced the solution: he had located a copy of the work in Göttweig (with an additional measure at the beginning) bearing an ascription to Witt. The initials "P.F.W." on the first violin probably stood for *per Friderico Witt*.[23] Stein attempted to renew his case for Beethoven's authorship on stylistic grounds,[24] but Ralph Leavis has pointed out convincingly that the "Beethovenian" passages in the work are actually the ones most closely modeled on moments in Haydn symphonies, including several works antedating the London visits.[25] Furthermore, a third copy of the work has been located in Rudolstadt, and it also is ascribed to Witt.[26] Witt had as much opportunity to know the Haydn symphonies of 1791–1792 as Beethoven, and he was actively engaged in composing and performing symphonies at the time the work was presumably written, late 1792 or shortly thereafter. In view of the strength of the documentary evidence for Witt's authorship, there seems no reasonable basis for ascribing the work to anyone else.

[20] Fritz Stein, "Eine unbekannte Jugendsymphonie Beethovens?" *Sammelbände der internationalen Musikgesellschaft* XIII (1911/1912) 127–72.

[21] Kinsky-Halm, *Beethoven*, 713–14.

[22] Robert Simpson, "Observations on the 'Jena' symphony," *The music survey* II (1949/1950) 155–60.

[23] H. C. Robbins Landon, "The 'Jena' symphony," *Essays on the Viennese classical style* (London: Barrie & Rockliff, 1970) 152–59; the original publication was in *The music review* XVIII (1957) 109–13.

[24] Fritz Stein, "Zum Problem der 'Jenaer Symphonie,' " *Bericht über den siebenten internationalen musikwissenschaftlichen Kongress Köln 1958* (Kassel: Bärenreiter, 1959) 279–81.

[25] Ralph Leavis, "Die 'Beethovenianismen' der Jenaer Symphonie," *Die Musikforschung* XXIII (1970) 297–302.

[26] This copy, from the former Schwarzburg-Rudolstadt collection, also lacks the first measure found in the Göttweig version.

# Symphonic works

The Thematic Index in this volume represents only a preliminary attempt to bring the Witt symphonies under bibliographic control. There are undoubtedly many additional sources for the works listed and there may well be more works than the twenty-three given there.

The works divide neatly into two groups, the nine symphonies published by André after 1800 and fourteen works found only in manuscript sources. In the numbering system employed in the Thematic Index, the published works come first in order to retain the numbering of the printed editions, which is presumably authentic. The unpublished symphonies have been arbitrarily assigned numbers 10–23. The establishment of a more satisfactory arrangement will require a more extensive bibliographical and stylistic investigation than has yet been possible. The published works are the later ones; most if not all the unpublished symphonies originated before 1800, many of them in the early 1790's when Witt was in residence at Wallerstein. The published works do not occur in sources prior to 1800; their relatively large scorings also suggest a later date.

Nearly all the unpublished symphonies occur in copies in South German collections, as one would expect if they were being distributed from the Wallerstein court. Copies of Them. Index 10–13 in the Wallerstein collection were made in 1790 and one of Them. Index 15 was made in 1793.[27] The Thurn und Taxis symphony catalogue shows that that court owned eight symphonies in the 1790's, Them. Index 11–13, 16–18, 22, and 23, although not all of them survive in the collection today.[28] Copies of Them. Index 11 and 19–21

in the Bayerische Staatsbibliothek may have come from the Hohenlohe-Bartenstein collection.[29] The Schönborn-Wiesentheid collection contains copies of Them. Index 10, 12, and 22. Only the "Jena" symphony (Them. Index 14) does not appear in at least one of these four collections. Of the sources for that work, the Göttweig copy is Viennese;[30] the provenance of the copy in Rudolstadt and of the copies of Them. Index 14 and 16 in Jena has yet to be determined (the latter two MSS appear to be rather poor textually).[31] Beyond this, there is a copy of Them. Index 15 in the former Mecklenburg collection in Schwerin, possibly due to the contact Witt had with that court in the late 1790's.[32]

Ironically, the only Witt symphonies heretofore available in modern editions were three juvenile works, Them. Index 12, 14, and 16, a situation that has made it difficult to evaluate Witt's achievement as a composer. A preliminary investigation of the later symphonies indicates that many features of Witt's style remained consistent throughout his career: he carries on much of the Wallerstein tradition with the addition of some Haydnesque features. The vast majority of Witt's symphonies are in four movements with an introduction (the one-movement work Them. Index 23 is perhaps an overture), a pattern typical of the Wallerstein school as well as of late

[27] See Haberkamp, *Oettingen-Wallerstein*, 214–15.

[28] The Thurn und Taxis symphony catalogue (full citation in the list of catalogue references below) seems to reflect the state of that collection about the end of the 1790's; on the present holdings of the collection see Gertraut Haberkamp, compiler, *Die Musikhandschriften der Fürst Thurn und Taxis Hofbibliothek Regensburg: Thematischer Katalog* (Munich: Henle, 1981) 367; the dates for MSS given there are only approximate.

[29] Information kindly supplied by Dr. Robert Münster.

[30] Landon, "'Jena' Symphony," 155–57.

[31] Based on an examination of the printed editions based on them. I suspect that Witt added an extra measure at the beginning of Them. Index 14 and that the Jena and Rudolstadt MSS represent an earlier textual state of the work than the one in Göttweig.

[32] Otto Kade, compiler, *Die Musikalien-Sammlung des Grossherzoglich Mecklenburg-Schweriner Fürstenhauses aus den letzten zwei Jahrhunderten*, 2 vols. (Schwerin: Sandmeyer, 1893) 313, lists this MS along with a dedication score of *Die Auferstehung Jesu* presented by Witt to the court and a few other items; I have no information about the present holdings of the collection in Schwerin.

Haydn.[33] Witt's melodic and harmonic vocabulary contains few surprises, and his handling of the standard formal designs is by and large straightforward. A glance at the Thematic Index will reveal Witt's fondness for foreshadowing the opening of his first allegro in the introduction to a symphony (see Them. Index 2, 7, 8, 15, and 16). The published symphonies appear to continue the line of development begun in the earlier ones, taking it to a more sophisticated level.

Of the three early symphonies presently available in print, the work in B-flat major (Them. Index 12) is probably the earliest, having been composed no later than 1790. It is a competent work, by and large, although exhibiting some peculiarities—in particular, the development section in the first movement is essentially a closed episode in the submediant. The "Jena" symphony (Them. Index 14) must date from 1792 or later, perhaps not much later. Its formal structures are more conventional—not surprisingly, considering how much of the first two movements is borrowed. The best of the early works currently in print is the A major symphony (Them. Index 16), a rather well-crafted piece that seems to show Witt's assimilation of some of the Haydnesque elements he was confronting in the "Jena."

The published series of nine symphonies can be dated in part with reference to André's edition numbers and the Whistling/Hofmeister catalogue.[34] The first eight works of the group ap-

peared in pairs at intervals of about two years from 1803/1804 to 1810/1811; the solitary No. 9 followed the others by about five years. Probably these symphonies were printed not long after their composition (the first pair perhaps excepted), as there seems to be no independent manuscript source tradition for any of them.[35] At least the latter works in the printed series must have been written for the Winterkonzerte in Würzburg; Witt's immediate audience had changed from a feudal setting to a middle-class one. His ultimate audience was, of course, now much wider—the Philharmonic Society of Bethlehem, Pennsylvania, for instance, owned copies of all nine of the printed symphonies. The *Allgemeine musikalische Zeitung* gives us some indication of the reception they had. A Leipzig performance of No. 1 in 1805 was reported with great enthusiasm.[36] Nos. 5 and 6 received extended and (at least for No. 5) highly favorable reviews on their publication.[37] Performances of Nos. 4 and 7 in the next few years were accorded more qualified praise.[38] Finally, a detailed review of No. 9 appears to summarize many aspects of Witt's symphonic career:

> He shows that he has diligently studied the works of the masters, and appears particularly to be following in the footsteps of Haydn. If one does not find in his works the rich imagination, the ever-youthful freshness, the living hue of his predecessor, if one might observe that the love of his model has perhaps held him back too much from the advances of recent times and thus given his works an old-fashioned appearance, one must recognize in him a significant talent, by which he gains the listener's interest through

---

[33] See Murray, *Seven symphonies*, xxi.

[34] On André's edition numbers, see Otto Erich Deutsch, *Musik-verlags Nummern* (Berlin: Merseburger, 1961) 6–7; Wolfgang Matthäus, "Das Werk Joseph Haydns im Spiegel der Geschichte des Verlages Jean André," *The Haydn yearbook* III (1965) 54–110. Symphonies No. 1–8 appear in C. F. Whistling, *Handbuch der musikalischen Literatur* (Leipzig: Meysel, 1817); No. 9 appears in the *Erster Nachtrag* (1818), which includes publications of 1816–1817.

Anomalies with the prints of Symphonies No. 1 and 2 might indicate that their publication history is more complex than that of the other seven. No. 1 appears with edition numbers 1886 and 1887, the latter number being also used for No. 2, and the copies with edition number 1887 have a second plate number 289. The first pages of the two violin I parts have an additional number 14 that is visible on the frontispiece to the score of No. 2 on page 2.

[35] The Göttweig copy of No. 2 is lost. The Witt MS in **B** Bc with call number 7960 consists of a few string parts to Symphonies No. 1 and 2 (description kindly supplied by Paul Raspé); probably these represent duplicates to copies of the prints no longer in the collection. A MS score of symphonies No. 5, 3, 8, and 4 in the Staats- und Universitätsbibliothek, Hamburg, signature MA I 1172, contains only chamber-music arrangements (my thanks to Dr. Bernhard Stockmann for this information).

[36] AMZ VIII (1805–1806) col. 225.

[37] AMZ XI (1808–1809) cols. 513–21.

[38] AMZ XII (1809–1810) col. 931; XIV (1812) col. 725.

skilled manipulation of his scarcely novel ideas and forms.[39]

Witt was thus commanding more respect than enthusiasm; tastes were changing and his popularity waning.

The later Witt symphonies show a few new features. Witt experiments with a variety of interesting scorings; although Kretzschmar's characterization of Witt as a "little Berlioz"[40] is an exaggera-

tion, one can see Witt's interest in exploring unusual sonorities in such places as the trios of the minuets of Symphonies No. 1 (horn II solo) and 2 (high cello solo), the slow movement of No. 7 (optional solo guitar), and the whole of No. 8 ("Turkish" instruments, four horns in different keys). Witt's harmonic language slowly expands in the last symphonies and his formal procedures become a bit less routine; the first movement of No. 9 has a recapitulation in which the opening material is greatly altered and abridged. Still, his works are decidedly conservative for their time.

[39] AMZ XXI (1819) cols. 607–11.

[40] Hermann Kretzschmar, *Führer durch den Concertsaal, I. Abtheilung: Sinfonie und Suite, I. Band* (Leipzig: Breitkopf & Härtel, 1898) 208.

# Symphony No. 2 in D major (Them. Index 2)

As this work was published in 1803/1804, it predates Witt's involvement with the Winterkonzerte and quite possibly his settling in Würzburg. Stylistically it seems to represent a point a bit further along in Witt's development than the A major symphony (Them. Index 16) discussed above. The wind scoring of this work is the lightest of the composer's later symphonies, calling for no clarinets and only one flute. Witt's frequent division of the violas is a feature of the Wallerstein style of orchestration.

The work begins with an extended introduction that presents the most important thematic idea of the first movement. In the first theme of the exposition proper, this idea occurs in the lower strings with a countermelody in the first violins; the passage is reminiscent of the corresponding place in Haydn's Symphony No. 91, I, 21–26:

Haydn, however, has constructed his theme in double counterpoint and proceeds to make good use of that fact. Witt's theme could be inverted

with the countermelody without great difficulty (in contrapuntal inversion Witt would avoid the awkward six-four chord in m. 31), but he seems unaware of the possibility. The theme itself is not very graceful, but it does provide a useful motivic idea that recurs throughout the exposition. The second theme and closing theme are new, contrasting ideas, but the initial motif of the first theme figures in the transitional passages preceding each of them. Witt begins the development with the opening idea from the exposition transposed to the dominant, an archaic procedure he abandoned later on in favor of more imaginative openings. The development continues by working out this thematic material, proceeding harmonically to the submediant by way of a colorful digression to the flat side. Witt's recapitulation is by and large mechanical, with a slight extension of the closing material to round off the movement. The one other spot that does not follow the exposition is measures 161ff., replacing part of the transition. This is a place where composers often engage in fresh developmental activity with considerable harmonic motion in order to set up the return of the second theme in the tonic as an important point of arrival; Charles Rosen terms this the "secondary development section."[41] Witt does develop his main motivic idea further in this passage, but he does not go far from the tonic and the part-writing here is rather careless. By late Classical standards this is a perfunctory approach to the recapitulation, and Witt seems to have moved toward more imaginative procedures later.

Although Witt at this stage in his career seems to have had his troubles with opening movements, the remainder of the symphony is more successful. The slow movement is a set of variations on a pretty but naive theme consisting of two repeated eight-measure phrases. Some of Haydn's variation themes are almost as naive-sounding, but Haydn usually has some means at hand of interrupting the symmetry of the theme before it becomes deadly (e.g., the "surprise" in the slow movement of Symphony No. 94). Witt evidently recognized the problem, but his solution is not as elegant as one might wish: he adds a little transitional passage in measures 33–42 to link the theme to the first variation. Once the variations

get under way, he manages more successfully, and the movement concludes with a long coda that moves well to the flat side of the tonic before the end. The minuet is rhythmically vigorous; the melody of the trio is entrusted to a solo cello (Witt's instrument) playing in a high register with the first oboe doubling at the octave. The finale is a sonata-form movement on a slightly smaller scale than the first movement. The movement is "monothematic"; that is, the second theme is derived from the first, in this instance reworked from the same elements rather than literally repeated. The development modulates away from the dominant immediately in up-to-date fashion. The recapitulation follows its expected course, but in a shorter movement a literal recapitulation is less of a problem than it is in a longer one. The symphony ends pianissimo, as is only appropriate for a basically lyrical work. The overall impression the symphony gives of Witt is that he was a facile composer who had the knack for finding attractive thematic material and who did not overreach himself in striving for any unusual depth of expression.

[41] Charles Rosen, *Sonata forms* (New York: Norton, 1980) 104.

## Editorial method

This score of Witt's Symphony No. 2 was prepared as a conductor's score by the Fleisher Collection using the André edition of the parts as a source. The notation has been tacitly modernized. Editorial additions of accidentals, dynamics, and groups of staccato marks have been indicated by brackets; added slurs and ties are indicated by a vertical slash through them. Inconsistencies in parallel passages have on occasion been altered to

bring parts into conformity with one another, but some have been allowed to stand. The variant notation of the ornamental figure in the melody of the trio of the minuet is instructive: the notation of the cello gives the realization of the trill in the oboe. Similarly the turn in the melodic parts in measure 22 of the second movement is an abbreviation for the grace-note figure that first appears in measure 6.

## Bibliography

Gerber, Ernst Ludwig. *Neues historisch-biographisches Lexikon der Tonkünstler*. 4 vols. Leipzig: Kühnel, 1812–1814. IV, cols. 593–94.

Kaul, Oskar. "Witt, Friedrich," *Die Musik in Geschichte und Gegenwart*, ed. Friedrich Blume. 16 vols. Kassel: Bärenreiter, 1949–1979. XIV, cols. 740–41.

Landon, H. C. Robbins. "The 'Jena' symphony," *Essays on the Viennese classical style*. London: Barrie & Rockliff, 1970. 152–59. An earlier version appeared in *The music review* XVIII (1957) 109–13.

Leavis, Ralph. "Die 'Beethovenianismen' der Jenaer Symphonie," *Die Musikforschung* XXIII (1970) 297–302.

———. "Witt, Friedrich," *The new Grove dictionary of music and musicians*, ed. Stanley Sadie. 20 vols. London: Macmillan, 1980. XX, 466–67.

Schiedermair, Ludwig. "Die Blütezeit der Öttingen-Wallerstein'schen Hofkapelle," *Sammelbände der internationalen Musikgesellschaft* IX (1907/1908) 83–130.

Simpson, Robert. "Observations on the 'Jena' symphony," *The music survey* II (1949/1950) 155–60.

Stein, Fritz. "Eine unbekannte Jugendsymphonie Beethovens?" *Sammelbände der internationalen Musikgesellschaft* XIII (1911/1912) 127–72.

———. "Zum Problem der 'Jenaer Symphonie,'" *Bericht über den siebenten internationalen musikwissenschaftlichen Kongress Köln 1958*. Kassel: Bärenreiter, 1959. 279–81.

Zobeley, Fritz. "Vorbemerkung," *Friedrich Witt: Symphonie B-dur* (Them. Index 12). Wiesbaden: Breitkopf & Härtel, 1968.

# Antoine Reicha

## *Life and works*

This cosmopolitan figure could be claimed as either a Czech or a German, and he spent an important part of his career in Vienna, but his most significant accomplishments came while he was resident in France. For that reason it seems most appropriate to use the French form of his name. Reicha was born in Prague on 26 February 1770. His father, a musician, died before Antoine was a year old, and after his mother's remarriage the boy's education seems to have been neglected. About the age of ten he took matters into his own hands by running away to join his grandfather in Klatovy. Grandfather Reicha decided to send Antoine to live with his uncle Joseph Reicha, cellist and composer at the Wallerstein court, and it was at Wallerstein that Antoine began his musical education.[42] Conceivably Witt was around the court while the Reichas were there. Certainly when Joseph Reicha took up a new post at the electoral court in Bonn in 1785, Antoine found a

friend in another musically talented boy born in the same year as he, Ludwig van Beethoven. Reicha's not altogether reliable autobiographical sketch tells us, "We spent fourteen years together; a second Orestes and Pylades, we could not be separated in our youth."[43] Although in fact they were together for only seven years in Bonn, there is no reason to doubt that Beethoven and Reicha were friends. Reicha had learned to play the violin and flute well enough to join the orchestra and he began composing as well. Beethoven played the viola in Reicha's first symphony, which he completed at the age of seventeen.[44] Beethoven and Reicha matriculated together at the University of Bonn in 1789. Beethoven did not carry his studies very far, but Reicha applied himself with great enthusiasm to learning philosophy and mathe-

[42] See Murray, *Seven symphonies*, particularly score 5, Joseph Reicha's Symphony D1.

[43] Antoine Reicha, *Notes sur Antoine Reicha*, ed. Jiří Vysloužil (Brno: Opus musicum, 1970) 44. The more significant portions of this autobiographical sketch appear in English translation in J. G. Prod'homme, "From the unpublished autobiography of Antoine Reicha," *The musical quarterly* XXII (1936) 339–53.

[44] Reicha, *Notes*, 16, 48.

matics. His speculative and didactic bent was to be obvious throughout the rest of his career. Reicha and Beethoven met Haydn in Bonn as Haydn was on his way to London in December 1790 and again on Haydn's return trip in July 1792. A few months later Beethoven departed for Vienna to study with Haydn; Reicha remained in Bonn with his uncle.

The musical and political situation in Bonn was deteriorating due to the French revolutionary wars and the ill health of both the Elector and Joseph Reicha. In late 1794 Antoine left for Hamburg just ahead of a French invasion. Joseph Reicha died shortly thereafter. Antoine gave up performing and for the rest of his life made his living primarily as a teacher, engaging in speculative and compositional activities in his free hours. He met Haydn again in August 1795 as Haydn was returning from his second London visit. Reicha began to send his works to publishers during the Hamburg years. A letter to the Viennese publisher Artaria of 1 October 1797 explains that he has been composing for twelve years but has waited until now to publish because he wanted to be satisfied that his works were good; they are "entirely written in the style [Geschmack] of Mozart." Reicha enclosed a three-page list of his compositions, some of which had already been bought by Pleyel in Paris.[45] Although Artaria did not take Reicha up on his offer, other publishers were to issue dozens of Reicha's works in the course of the next quarter century.

In 1799 Reicha went to Paris hoping to have an opera performed there. This plan ultimately came to nothing, but he did have symphonies performed at the Concerts des amateurs and at the Opéra. These symphonies traditionally have been identified as Opp. 41 and 42, which Breitkopf published some four years later.

From late 1801 to late 1808 Reicha resided in Vienna. He renewed his acquaintance with Haydn and studied with Albrechtsberger and Salieri. Reicha also resumed his friendship with Beethoven. A letter from Beethoven to his friend Zmeskall written in November 1802 invites the latter to a musical get-together with Reicha.[46] Carl van Beethoven, who was at times his brother's business agent, also conducted some negotiations on Reicha's behalf with Breitkopf & Härtel, offering them a group of works on 22 January 1803, including three symphonies for the price of sixty ducats.[47] Presumably two of these were Opp. 41 and 42. Prince Lobkowitz had Reicha's opera L'ouragan performed privately at his palace and probably also had orchestral works by Reicha played by his orchestra; a set of parts to Reicha's Symphonie concertante in E minor for two cellos and orchestra survives in the former Lobkowitz collection.[48] (The work begins with a theme that first appears to be in C major, only settling into E minor after several measures; whether Reicha wrote it before Beethoven used the same device in the finale of his E minor quartet, Op. 59, No. 2, cannot be determined.)

Reicha's most famous publications in these years were works of at least partly didactic nature. His Trente-six fugues pour le piano-forte composées d'après un nouveau système, published in 1803, aroused a controversy. Reicha demonstrated in these works a variety of novel approaches to the fugue, including the use of intervals of imitation other than the fourth and fifth and of unusual meters including both quintuple and septuple time. The work was dedicated to Haydn and undoubtedly represents in part the result of discussions with Haydn and the other musicians Reicha knew in Vienna; Beethoven complained about

[45] Described and quoted in Rosemary Hilmar, Der Musikverlag Artaria & Comp. (Tutzing: Hans Schneider, 1977) 39–40; the letter is in the Wiener Stadt- und Landesbibliothek.

[46] Anderson, 66; KK, 70.

[47] Ernst Bücken, Anton Reicha: sein Leben und seine Kompositionen (Munich: C. Wolf, 1912) 39, n. 1.

[48] CS Pnm X. g. e. 88; for incipits, see Šotolová, Rejcha, 137. The Lobkowitz orchestra included the fine father-and-son team of cellists Anton and Nikolaus Kraft.

the work in a letter written to Breitkopf & Härtel that seems to predate its publication.[49] Reicha's *Practische Beispiele*, also published in 1803, contains further examples of his rhythmic and harmonic innovations. Prince Louis Ferdinand offered Reicha a post as his teacher, with the promise of a permanent position when one became available at the Prussian court. Reicha declined the offer but dedicated his next speculative work, *L'art de varier*, a set of fifty-seven variations for piano, to the prince in 1804.

Reicha's later years in Vienna may have been less propitious than the earlier ones. Artistic differences may have cooled his friendship with Beethoven somewhat. Although Reicha and Beethoven shared a number of common preoccupations, including the exploration of new territory in the fugue and the set of variations (consider the finale of the "Eroica"), they may not have been in sympathy with each other's work in these areas. Maurice Emmanuel has pointed to the lack of reference to Reicha in the Beethoven correspondence after 1803 and to the lack of reference to Beethoven in Reicha's treatises as indications of this.[50] Reicha did continue to see Haydn, introducing Cherubini and Baillot to the old master when they visited Vienna in 1805. His position in Vienna may never have been altogether satisfactory, however, and in 1808, as a war between France and Austria was brewing, Reicha decided to try his luck in Paris again.

From late 1808 until his death in 1836, Reicha was a major figure in Parisian musical life. His Symphony No. 3 in F major (Score 3), composed in Vienna the preceding summer, was premiered successfully in a concert at the Conservatoire on 7 May 1809. Three of Reicha's operas were produced for short runs beginning with *Cagliostro* in 1810; *Natalie* followed in 1816, and finally *Sapho* in 1822.

Reicha's quintets for flute, oboe, clarinet, bassoon, and horn, dating from about 1811 to 1820, were phenomenally popular for a time and have become a cornerstone of the modern wind quintet repertory with the revival of interest in this ensemble in recent decades. Reicha seems to have composed relatively little after the early 1820's. His greatest accomplishments were as a teacher and theorist, whose numerous counterpoint pupils included some of the leading musicians of Paris. His *Traité de mélodie* appeared in 1814, and another major treatise, *Cours de composition musicale*, was published a few years later. In 1818 Reicha was appointed professor of counterpoint and fugue at the Conservatoire, where eight of his pupils were already teaching. Although by this time Reicha's approach to the subject had become more traditional, the next years were enlivened by controversies among the adherents of Reicha, Cherubini, and Fétis. Also in 1818 Reicha married Virginie Enaust; they had two daughters. Reicha's most important theoretical work, the *Traité de haute composition musicale*, appeared in 1824–1826; a last major treatise, the *Art du compositeur dramatique*, was published in 1833. Reicha was naturalized as a French citizen in 1829 and became a chevalier of the Légion d'honneur in 1831. In 1835 he crowned his career with his entry into the Académie des beaux-arts. The next year he caught a chill while attending a session of the Académie and died on 28 May 1836. His pupils had included Adam, Onslow, Gounod, Franck, Berlioz, and Liszt; his writings had been widely translated and reprinted.

Berlioz, who had begun studying with Reicha at the Conservatoire in 1826, described Reicha and Lesueur as his "two masters." He praised Reicha's teaching for its clarity and found him exceptionally devoted to the welfare of his students. He recalled also Reicha's opinion that the study of mathematics had given him the self-discipline needed to master his ideas, but suggested instead that Reicha's failure to make an

---

[49]Anderson, 77; *KK*, 71.

[50]Maurice Emmanuel, *Antonin Reicha* (Paris: Renouard, 1937) 11.

enduring mark as a composer might have been the lack of musical spontaneity that Reicha's theorizing had brought about.[51]

A further aspect of Reicha's career that should be noted is the contrast between his speculative works and the works written for more general consumption. To Gerber the contrast between Reicha's conservative and radical aspects was so striking that he devoted two separate articles to him in the *Neues historisch-biographisches Lexikon der Tonkünstler* under the impression that he was dealing with two different men![52] In the symphonies in particular one finds that there are movements and works with few innovative features (such as the work in C minor, Score 2) and

others with a great many (Op. 42). Many of Reicha's most interesting ideas were not used by him to any great extent, some not at all. Berlioz developed further some of Reicha's ideas, notably those on augmented orchestral scoring, but other aspects of Reicha's work—rhythmic and metrical innovations, suggested alternatives to the major-minor scale system including quarter tones, and incipient polytonality—did not enter the vocabulary of Western music until much later, and Reicha's role in bringing these things to pass was probably not great. His theoretical works, however, are also immensely valuable for the insights they give on the practice of his day. His music has also come to have a place in the present-day repertory, although principally the chamber music with winds, not necessarily the most innovative part of his oeuvre in any respect other than scoring.

[51] Hector Berlioz, *Mémoires*, ed. Pierre Citron, 2 vols. (Paris: Garnier-Flammarion, 1969) 97–100.

[52] Ernst Ludwig Gerber, *Neues historisch-biographisches Lexikon der Tonkünstler*, 4 vols. (Leipzig: Kühnel, 1812–1814) III, cols. 811–13.

## Symphonic works

As a glance at the recent Reicha thematic catalogue by Olga Šotolová[53] or the work list by Peter Eliot Stone[54] will reveal, there are still many bibliographical questions to be answered about Reicha's symphonies. At least nine symphonies for full orchestra survive complete or in fragments, but Reicha's output probably numbered over a dozen. Some of the missing works may be irretrievably lost, but until a more thorough search for sources has been made, it will not be possible to give more than a preliminary idea of Reicha's oeuvre. Even the best-known group of Reicha sources, the manuscripts in the old Conservatoire collection in Paris, needs to be investigated with regard to such matters as chronology.

Besides the two scores in this series, only three symphonies survive complete in the sources so far examined, the two published works and a Symphony in F minor.[55] None of these symphonies can be dated precisely.

The two symphonies published by Breitkopf & Härtel as Opp. 41 and 42 are the only Reicha symphonies to have achieved any wide distribution. Both have been published in modern editions.[56] Traditionally they have been assigned the publication date of 1803, although the *Allgemeine musikalische Zeitung* did not review them (with an apology for lateness, to be sure) until 1808. (The

[53] Šotolová, *Rejcha*; the symphonies appear on 139–46 (the last work, which is for wind orchestra, has not been considered here).

[54] Peter Eliot Stone, "Reicha, Antoine(-Joseph)," *Grove* XV, 696–702; this also contains the most recent full bibliography.

[55] Paris, Bibliothèque nationale, Ms. 14501, a set of autograph parts with string duplicates by a French copyist.

[56] The score of Op. 41 appeared in the series Musica antiqua bohemica, No. 76, ed. Vratislav Bělský (Prague: Supraphon, 1973). A performing edition of Op. 42 is available from Edwin F. Kalmus (Miami, n.d.). Performance material for both Opp. 41 and 42 is available from the Edwin A. Fleisher Collection, Free Library of Philadelphia, Philadelphia, PA 19103, Nos. 4104 and 4105 respectively.

review, on the whole favorable, found them marred by a tendency to strive for the bizarre.)[57] Although the works have been identified at times with the symphonies Reicha gave in Paris a few years earlier, this is conjectural.

The two Reicha symphonies for which autograph dates exist both come from 1808. Symphony No. 1 in G major is dated "Vienne le 13 Juil. 1808";[58] Symphony No. 3 in F major is dated "Vienne le 14 Sept. 1808." No Symphony No. 2 can be identified to go with them. Unfortunately, the autograph of the G major symphony is incomplete. Although the score of the F major symphony is intact, Reicha added an introduction on a separate bifolio at a later date, possibly just before the work received its first performance in Paris the following spring (see the description below); the date is therefore not as final as one would wish. (The autograph fragment of Op. 41 shows that the introduction to that work was also an afterthought.[59])

The two remaining symphonies for which we have complete sources can both be associated with Paris. As will be discussed below, the autograph of the *Symphonie à petit orchestre* No. 1 in C minor is on French paper and must have been written in Paris. French duplicate string parts to the Symphony in F minor indicate at least a performance in Paris, although that tells us nothing about the time of composition of the work.

Reicha's symphonies are cast in the usual late Classical four-movement design.[60] His choice of key relationships among the movements is likewise conventional for the most part (placing the slow movement of his F minor symphony in C major is his one unusual choice among the works

examined). Reicha's individuality becomes evident, however, as one looks in more detail at the form of the separate movements.

As Reicha was one of the theorists who established the nineteenth-century concept of sonata form (or, as Reicha terms it, *la grande coupe binaire*), it is instructive to consider his first movements in the light of his descriptions of the form in the *Traité de mélodie* and the *Traité de haute composition musicale*.[61] About half the discussion in the *Traité de mélodie* concerns the tonal plan of the movement. Reicha insists that the only allowable secondary key in a major-mode piece is the dominant, as any other choice will weaken the tonic, and only certain unnamed bad composers will attempt to make their weak musical ideas seem better by introducing heterogeneous modulations. (To say the least, Reicha was out of sympathy with Beethoven on this issue.) In the minor mode, the possible secondary keys are the dominant and relative major. In the first movements of the major-mode symphonies under discussion, Reicha invariably goes to the dominant, and in the two minor-mode first movements, he goes to the relative major (the most usual choice, although Reicha does not say this).

The remainder of the discussion in the *Traité de mélodie* and all that in the *Traité de haute composition musicale* deal with the movement at a finer structural level. In the earlier treatise, Reicha states that the movement consists of (a) a theme defining the tonic; (b) a modulatory passage establishing the dominant and possibly further material; and (c) a second section, beginning with modulatory passages and then returning to the tonic for the restatement of the material of the first half of the movement in that key; this section composes and develops the material of the first half. In the decade between the two treatises,

---

[57] AMZ XI (1808–1809) cols. 129–135. A brief reference to a performance of an unidentified Reicha symphony in Leipzig in late 1803 appears on AMZ VI (1803–1804) col. 203; it "seems rather materials for a symphony than a symphony."

[58] Paris, Bibliothèque nationale, Ms. 14501.

[59] Paris, Bibliothèque nationale, Ms. 13107.

[60] Bücken, *Reicha*, 131, finds some cyclic elements in Op. 42, but these do not seem to be of great significance.

[61] Antoine Reicha, *Traité de mélodie*, 2 vols.: I, text; II, plates (second edition, Paris: A. Farrenc, 1832) I, 41–43; *Traité de haute composition musicale* (second edition, Paris: A. Farrenc, [ca. 1833]) 296–300.

Reicha refined his ideas quite a bit; although he may well have written no new symphonies, he can better describe his old ones. There is no preliminary discussion of the structure; instead Reicha sums it up in a diagram at the end.[62] Where in the earlier discussion Reicha had emphasized harmony, he now places harmonic and thematic elements on an approximately equal footing. Much of later sonata-form terminology is creeping into his discussion, at least descriptively; Reicha refers to the first part of the movement as an exposition and to the first subsection of the second half as a development.

Using an example in D major, Reicha discusses the important structural features of a movement as they come. His treatment of the first theme (*motif*) consists mainly of instructions on constructing a regular period. The transition (*pont*) should go to the dominant of A as the best way of establishing A as the new tonic (Reicha now indicates that in a minor-mode movement the more usual secondary key is the relative major). Reicha gives four possible chord progressions for use as short transitions; longer ones "should modulate incessantly and traverse many different keys." This last recommendation is not so much a reflection of Classical practice as it is of Reicha's own. Transitions in Haydn and Mozart usually have clear goals; Reicha's by comparison are hyperkinetic. Perhaps the extreme case occurs in the first movement of Op. 41, which very nearly establishes D as a tonal center in a movement in E-flat major; only a fairly elaborate second modulation gets us to B-flat. It is difficult to hear B-flat as the dominant after this. The transition in the first movement of the F major symphony is short but equally furious. It moves from F major in measure 80 abruptly into C minor and D minor, reaching a cadence on E in measure 91, and this E is reinterpreted as the third degree of the C major scale in measure 95 (Reicha's prescription of a half

[62] Reproduced in William S. Newman, *The sonata since Beethoven* (New York: Norton, 1972) 33, after a bilingual (French-German) version by Carl Czerny.

cadence in the new key does not apply here). In Haydn and Mozart one tends to hear the transitions as being logical outcomes of the first themes. Reicha's abrupt procedures seem less satisfactory and may well be one of the reasons the contemporary critics found his works bizarre. The effect is enhanced by Reicha's use of new thematic material (he says merely that the transition should employ accessory ideas) with wide leaps and greatly increased rhythmic activity and his use of extremes in dynamics and texture. For the second theme Reicha specifies a periodic structure. The last part of the exposition should consist of accessory ideas, short motifs or eight-measure phrases, and may modulate but must conclude in A. Reicha's actual practice is better described by the later notion of a transition to closing and a closing theme.

Although Reicha states that the second part of the movement can be two or three times the length of the first, the sonata-form movements in his symphonies have rather short development sections and do not approach this ratio. Reicha makes no specific recommendations about what material to use in the development; he states that a new idea may be introduced here, although the place where new ideas are most necessary is in the coda. New thematic ideas appear at the beginning of the development in the first movements of both works in this series; in fact, the entire development of the first movement of the C minor work consists of a statement of a new theme. Reicha's development sections frequently use material from the transitions, often continuing harmonic processes initiated there as well. Reicha considers the development and what we call the retransition to be coequal elements in the hierarchy of the form, and in fact they do not always differ appreciably in length.

The second section of the second part of the movement (Reicha does not use the term *recapitulation*) begins with the first theme in the tonic; part of it may appear in another key, such as the subdominant. The following passage, replacing the transition, should modulate and then re-establish the tonic. From this point the material originally heard in the dominant should recur in the tonic, but Reicha is emphatic that this should not be a mechanical transposition. In works "of our day" that procedure is not followed; instead, one should: alter the order of ideas; change the scoring, texture, or harmony of sections; vary the melody; or add developmental passages. The movement ends with "an interesting coda." In general in Classical sonata forms one finds that a recapitulation with greatly reordered thematic material will stay close to the tonic (many of Haydn's) and that one with colorful harmonic turns will preserve the general order of events from the exposition to maintain coherence (as in many of Mozart's). Reicha usually follows this pattern. The themes in the first-movement recapitulation in the F minor symphony have been reshuffled and much of the material has been shifted from major to minor, but harmonically this recapitulation is the most straightforward of the six. The other five recapitulations examined tend to leave the tonic for long stretches. This is not just a matter of having secondary development sections or developmental passages toward the end of the movement: in each movement one of the thematic statements is out of the tonic. The recapitulations of the first movements of Op. 42 and of the C minor symphony begin in the subdominant, as Reicha allows in his discussion (the most famous example of a subdominant recapitulation occurs in the first movement of Mozart's piano

sonata, K. 545). In the F major and G major symphonies a later section of the recapitulation appears in the subdominant, transposed down a major second from its first statement; in the G major symphony this stretch includes the second theme (earlier examples of this transposition appear in the first movement of Haydn's Symphony No. 71 and the finale of Beethoven's Op. 21). The procedure in the first movement of Op. 41 is even more striking: after the secondary development section has reached a tonic cadence in E-flat major, the second theme appears in C minor. Reicha uses the term *coda* in his discussion to refer to all the material following the second theme in the recapitulation; except for the short concluding passage in the first movement of the C minor symphony he does not add a substantial new section after the end of the recapitulation proper in any of these movements. With regard to minor-key movements in general, the *Traité de mélodie* indicates that such a movement may end in major but that one should make certain not to spoil the character of the piece. In the *Traité de haute composition musicale* Reicha advises against transposing the second theme into the minor. Both minor-key first movements under consideration end in the minor; in the C minor work just mentioned Reicha recapitulates the second theme and following material in C major and adds the coda to restore the minor mode, while in the F minor symphony he stays in minor throughout the recapitulation.

## The two symphonies in this series
### Symphonie à petit orchestre No. 1 in C minor

The autograph, Paris, Bibliothèque nationale, Ms. 14500, is not dated; despite the "No. 1" in the title no other works of this type are known. The manuscript measures 30 by 23 cm. and consists of twenty folios. The core, folios 3–18, consists of

three gatherings of six, six, and four folios on French paper (watermark: heart and the word BERGE[R?] on a scroll; countermark: bunch of eight grapes in four ranks, 2, 3, 2, 1, with cross and F below); this paper is ruled with sixteen staves. The music begins on folio 3r. Folios 2 and 19 consist of a single sheet wrapped around the core; the watermark is the same but the paper is ruled with twenty staves. Folio 2 is bare of music. Folios 1 and 20 are a wrapper around the rest of the manuscript on unlined paper of a different French type (watermark: F; countermark: shell). The work must have been composed during one of Reicha's periods in Paris, either in 1799–1801 or after 1808. By and large this is a fair copy; the only compositional alterations evident are changes to the ends of the strains of the minuet and the addition of three measures at the very end of the symphony.[63]

The title page informs us that the winds are *ad libitum*. Normally they function merely to reinforce the strings (but cf. the flute at m. 149ff. and the bassoons at m. 185ff. of the first movement). The work is restricted in scale as well as scoring. The introduction is a perfunctory six measures of unison. The first movement tends to avoid regular periodic structures and unambiguous sectional demarcations; for instance, the first point of articulation in the secondary key of E-flat major is a cadence on the subdominant in m. 31. The transition is short and direct. After the second theme Reicha reintroduces the opening idea in the transition to closing. After the double bar a new theme appears in E-flat major; the F minor passage that follows measures 86ff. is probably best heard as a subdominant beginning to the recapitulation in which the opening theme has been extended. The replacement passage for the transition ends with a half cadence; what follows is a return in C major of the new theme that took the place of the development section. The second theme and most of the following material reappear in C major. Only at the very end of the movement does C minor reassert itself with a final restatement of the

opening idea. The opening theme is thus stated five times (ignoring the repetition of the exposition) successively in C minor, E-flat major, F minor, C major, and C minor to function rather as a ritornello. With the comparative lack of developmental and transitional passages and the lack of periodicity of the thematic material, this gives the movement some decidedly un-Classical aspects.

The *Andante* is in the form ABCBA coda, with the sections being in E-flat major, C minor, C major, C minor, and E-flat major again. The minuet is in C minor and the finale in C major (by comparison, in the F minor symphony the minuet is in F major and the finale begins in F minor and concludes in major). The last movement may be the best. In the counterstatement of the opening theme Reicha introduces a new motif in the violins (m. 9, second half) that proceeds to take on a life of its own and get the transition under way rhythmically. The transition itself is less fantastic than, say, the one in the first movement of Op. 41, reaching G major by way of a thrust toward E minor. Following the second theme there is a brief turn toward the minor before the closing material reaffirms the major mode. The development takes up the melodic and harmonic material of the transition, with an initial drive toward E minor that is rapidly effaced by further modulations. After a relatively long retransition, the recapitulation begins in measure 116 with a C major version of the material that originally appeared in the minor following the second theme. This replaces the first eight measures of the exposition; everything after that follows in straightforward fashion.

Despite the associations of the minor mode with a highly dramatic style in much of the music of this period this little symphony does not seem to strive for any extraordinary depth of pathos. The return to C minor after the recapitulation of the first movement is somewhat reminiscent of Beethoven's Op. 67 (conceivably Reicha's work is earlier), but this symphony is so different in character that comparisons seem to have little point.

---

[63] Descriptions of the two symphony autographs kindly supplied by Catherine Massip; I have not examined either in person. The bunch of grapes resembles one illustrated in Jan LaRue, "Watermarks and musicology," *Acta musicologica* XXXIII (1961) 136, dated 1802.

## Symphony No. 3 in F major

The autograph, Paris, Bibliothèque nationale Ms. 14499, is in two pieces. The main body of the work is on a single gathering of twenty folios of Austrian paper (watermark: CAUZEN beneath a lily; countermark: FRANTZ & DANIEN) measuring 36.5 by 23.5 cm., ruled with twenty staves. The introduction is on one bifolio of French paper (watermark: I. ANDRIEU over AC; countermark: bunch of grapes) with fourteen staves, measuring 23 by 30 cm. (For technical reasons the introduction has been reproduced here in a diplomatic transcription rather than from the original.) Reicha has dated the score "Vienne le 4. Sept. 1808" and added the note, "Executée pour la première fois au Conservatoire de Musique à Paris le 7 mai 1809." The 1808 date certainly applies only to the body of the work; the introduction must date from after Reicha's arrival in Paris at the end of that year. Possibly the introduction was added for the first performance. As with the C minor symphony, this score is largely fair copy, but Reicha has made substantial changes to the end of the slow movement (the addition of m. 417–18 in the finale seems to be just the rectification of an error).

This is a larger and more ambitious work than the C minor symphony. Its first performance was a decided success; the *Allgemeine musikalische Zeitung* reports that it "afforded much enjoyment, at least as much as a symphony by such a composer can afford beside the masterworks this genre already possesses."[64] The orchestral writing in this symphony is fully in accordance with the norms of the period and of the other Reicha symphonies; although it is rarely virtuosic it does treat all the wind instruments as *obbligato* and gives the wind section a few passages without support from the strings (one such occurs in m. 318ff. of the first movement, a passage added to the recapitulation with no parallel in the exposition).

Several of the most striking features of the first movement have been discussed already in connection with Reicha's theoretical precepts. The long, elaborate introduction contrasts completely with the tiny one of the C minor symphony. As in the first movement of the C minor symphony the development begins with a new theme, but this one gives way to a working-out of the transition material and a substantial retransition. The new theme does not recur in this movement.

The C major triadic figure that begins the second movement was a favorite of Reicha's. The identical figure begins the C major slow movement of the F minor symphony, which continues differently. Furthermore, Reicha used this figure as the basis for an example of an eight-measure phrase in the *Traité de mélodie*;[65] his procedures in the symphonic slow movements are much more elaborate. The slow movement of this symphony is in sonata form, complete with a development; the result of all Reicha's surgery to the last part of the movement is a regular recapitulation.

The minuet is enormous: 162 measures, plus another 40 for the trio. The finale is also large—504 measures—although it lacks repetition signs. The very opening, in long notes without accompaniment, suggests that the movement will be contrapuntal; although this first idea does not recur in the exposition, many of the succeeding thematic elements are in fact handled contrapuntally. The opening motif comes into its own in the development, where it is treated fugally. The beginning of the recapitulation is also greatly expanded to develop this idea further, and near the end of the symphony the same motif reappears in stretto.

In the section of the *Traité de haute composition musicale* discussed earlier, Reicha emphasizes the need to have good thematic ideas. In evaluating this symphony, and Reicha's others, one must

[64]AMZ XI (1808–1809) col. 750.

[65]*Traité de mélodie* II, 2.

remark that much of his thematic material is rather commonplace. A further flaw in these works is the tendency for things to happen too abruptly and for bland passages to alternate with highly agitated ones with the effect of disruption more than cumulation. Still, these works are rarely dull for just this reason; if they say nothing profound, they are generally entertaining. Reicha's contribution to the symphony is not as important as his work as a theorist, but his symphonies deserve more attention than they have previously received.

## Bibliography

Bücken, Ernst. *Anton Reicha: sein Leben und seine Kompositionen.* Munich: C. Wolf, 1912.

Emmanuel, Maurice. *Antonin Reicha.* Paris: Renouard, 1937.

Reicha, Antoine. *Notes sur Antoine Reicha.* Edited and with Czech translation by Jiří Vysloužil. Brno: Opus musicum, 1970.

Šotolová, Olga. *Antonín Rejcha.* Prague: Supraphon, 1977.

Stone, Peter Eliot. "Reicha, Antoine(-Joseph)," *The new Grove dictionary of music and musicians*, ed. Stanley Sadie. 20 vols. London: Macmillan, 1980. XV, 696–702.

# Anton Eberl

## Life and works

To be sure, this new work of Beethoven's has great and bold ideas and, as one would expect from the genius of this composer, a tremendous power of execution; but the symphony would gain immeasurably (it lasts a full hour) if Beethoven could bring himself to shorten it and bring more light, clarity, and unity into the whole: qualities that Mozart's symphonies in G minor and C major, Beethoven's in C and D, and Eberl's in E-flat and D [minor], with all their wealth of ideas, interweavings of the instruments, and successions of surprising modulations, nowhere fail to reveal.[66]

So the regular Viennese correspondent of the *Allgemeine musikalische Zeitung* commented after hearing Beethoven conduct the first public performance of his third symphony at Franz Clement's concert at the Theater an der Wien on 7 April 1805. These comments and a few others like them by this critic have been frequently cited in the Beethoven literature as curiosities or as illustra-

Engraving of Eberl by Rahl after a portrait by Jagemann (Cologne, Stadt- und Universitätsbibliothek)

[66]AMZ VII (1804–1805) col. 501.

tions of the opposition that all true Romantic artists face from the philistines. It should not surprise us, however, that the "Eroica" daunted some (by no means all) of its early hearers; some others were even less sympathetic. Nor is it odd that the new symphony would be compared to Mozart's last two or Beethoven's first two, favorably or not. What does strike the modern reader as odd is the third member of the writer's symphonic trinity: not the still-living Joseph Haydn but Anton Eberl, the leading native Viennese composer of instrumental music of the younger generation. Again and again this critic uses Eberl and Beethoven, with the usual addition of Mozart and the occasional one of Haydn, as his standard in criticism of concertos and symphonies.[67] Furthermore, although this critic was probably Eberl's most enthusiastic supporter, he was far from alone in his opinion that Anton Eberl was a symphonist to be reckoned with.

Unlike Witt, Reicha, and Beethoven, Eberl was not the son of a professional musician; his father was a wealthy imperial official. This explains why Eberl, five years older than those three composers, was the last of this group to reach maturity as a symphonist. Eberl was born on 13 June 1765. He showed talent as a pianist early on, giving private performances at the age of eight. His family, however, insisted that he study jurisprudence in preparation for a career in government service. Only a financial crisis in the family prevented Eberl's taking his doctoral examinations and going on to a lifetime in the bureaucracy. Poor but free, Eberl was finally able to devote himself to music at some time in his late teens or early twenties. Anton's elder brother, Ferdinand (1762–1805), also broke with family tradition and in the 1780's began to make a career as a dramatist of the Viennese popular school. Ferdinand's best-known work was probably the libretto for Dittersdorf's *Betrug durch Aberglauben* (1786); he was to serve Anton as librettist on several occasions.

Although we do not know when Eberl began his musical career in earnest, 1783 seems at least to mark the beginning of a phase of considerable activity. This date appears on the libretto of his first Singspiel, *Die Marchande des Modes*; reportedly Gluck praised the work and urged the composer to seek more systematic theoretical instruction than he had had to that point. Eberl finished his first symphony, the one in D major (Them. Index w.o.n. [without opus number] 5) on 10 September of that year. On 9 January 1784 Eberl completed another symphony, the one in G major (Them. Index w.o.n. 6). Eberl gave an "Akademie" at the Burgtheater on 9 March 1784; except that he appeared as a pianist we have no information about the program, but these two works might well have been composed for it. The last and most accomplished of Eberl's three juvenile symphonies, the work in C major (Them. Index w.o.n. 7), was completed on 25 June 1785, less than two weeks after the composer's twentieth birthday. This work still shows technical deficiencies, but it establishes one aspect of Eberl's artistic orientation beyond doubt: the opening of the first movement is modeled on that of the "Haffner" symphony, K. 385, and from this time on Eberl may be counted among the followers of Mozart.

The precise degree of Eberl's contact with Mozart cannot be established. Eberl is not mentioned in the Mozart correspondence or other documents surviving from the Mozart circle from the older composer's lifetime. It is unlikely that Eberl was a direct pupil of Mozart. The two most reliable early biographical accounts, those by Gerber and the Viennese *Allgemeine musikalische Zeitung* correspondent speak of Eberl as a friend of Mozart's rather than as a pupil.[68] It was not until late in his career that Eberl achieved the technical assurance one would expect had he received the rigorous training that Mozart gave a Thomas Attwood. As late as 1800 Eberl would be criticized bitterly for inordinate lengthiness, faulty har-

---

[67] See *AMZ* VI (1803–1804) col. 621; VII (1804–1805) cols. 351, 470, 500; X (1807–1808) col. 140.

[68] Gerber, *Neues Lexikon* III, cols. 3–7; and necrology of Eberl, *AMZ* IX (1806–1807) cols. 423–30.

monic progressions, and poor voice-leading, and called "a man of talent and musical inventiveness who is however lacking a great deal—not merely what is called formal learning [*Schule*], but basic musical education [*Bildung*]."[69] Eberl did receive encouragement from Mozart, who reportedly used Eberl's variations on Ignaz Umlauf's *Zu Steffen sprach im Traume* (w.o.n. 2) as a teaching piece with his piano pupils. This work was close enough to Mozart in style to be published under Mozart's name in 1788, going through over a dozen later editions with the incorrect attribution despite the protests of the composer. It was only the first of a series of Eberl works, largely for piano, that appeared as Mozart in printed editions, the most recent of these being a 1944 publication of the Symphony in C major.[70]

Eberl composed no symphonies for nearly twenty years after the one in C major. In the late 1780's and early 1790's he wrote a good deal of piano music and a number of theatrical and vocal works. He composed a cantata, *Bey Mozarts Grab*, to a text by his brother, Ferdinand, within a week of Mozart's death, although the work seems never to have been performed. On 29 December 1794 at a concert at the Kärntnertortheater for the benefit of Constanze Mozart, Eberl performed a Mozart piano concerto between the acts of *La clemenza di Tito*. The evening was such a success that on the following 31 March there was another benefit performance of *Tito* with a Mozart piano concerto between the acts; the soloist on this occasion, however, was not Eberl but Beethoven. It was Eberl, though, who went on tour with Constanze and her sister Aloyisa Lange in late 1795 and early 1796. In the announcements of some of their appearances Eberl is given the title of Kapell-

meister, on what basis it is not certain,[71] but Eberl used it for the rest of his life. Eberl returned briefly to Vienna in 1796 and married Maria Anna Schefler on 28 March. Soon thereafter he took his bride to St. Petersburg, where he had been offered a post in one of the Russian noble households.

Eberl remained in Russia until the end of 1799; "Anton Eberl Music Meister in Petersburg" appeared on the list of subscribers to the first edition of Haydn's *Die Schöpfung*.[72] By this time Eberl was beginning to publish piano and chamber works. Many of these editions were dedicated to Russian patrons, including the violin-playing heir to the throne, Alexander Pavlovich (later Emperor Alexander I), who presented Eberl with a gold snuffbox as a reward for the dedication of the three piano trios, Op. 8. Eberl's greatest success in Russia came in October 1799 with the performance of his cantata *La gloria d'Imeneo*, composed for the marriage of Grand Duchess Alexandra Paulovna, daughter of Emperor Paul I, to Archduke Joseph of Austria, younger brother of Holy Roman Emperor Franz II. Eberl was later to use the overture to this cantata as a concert work.

In 1800 Eberl was back in Vienna, gathering acclaim for his Piano concerto in C major, Op. 32, which he had composed in St. Petersburg and premiered there in 1798.[73] On 23 May 1801 he brought forth two new stage works, the farce *Erwine von Steinheim* by Schikaneder's troupe at the Freihaustheater and, more importantly, the "romantisch grosse Zauber-Oper" *Die Königin der schwarzen Inseln* at the Kärntnertortheater. The

---

[69] AMZ III (1800–1801) col. 95; this is a review, with musical examples, of Eberl's Opp. 7–10.

[70] For a complete list, see Stephen C. Fisher, "Die C-dur Sinfonie KV Anh. C 11.14: ein Jugendwerk Anton Eberls," *Mitteilungen der internationalen Stiftung Mozarteum* (forthcoming).

[71] See Otto Erich Deutsch, *Mozart: die Dokumente seines Lebens* (Kassel: Bärenreiter, 1961) 412–16; Bauer, Deutsch, et al., eds., *Mozart: Briefe und Aufzeichnungen: Gesamtausgabe*, 6 vols. (Kassel: Bärenreiter, 1962–1975), No. 1216 (11 December 1795).

[72] Landon, *Haydn: chronicle and works* IV, 624.

[73] This follows the account in AMZ VIII (1805–1806) cols. 655–56 and 729; IX (1806–1807) col. 425. Johann Schwaldopler, *Historisches Taschenbuch mit besonderer Rücksicht auf die Österreichischen Staaten*, Jg. 1807 for 1803, places the work in 1803, but this may simply refer to a performance in that year (cited in White, "Eberl," 46, and Robert Haas, "Anton Eberl," *Mozart-Jahrbuch 1951*, 127–28).

latter was Eberl's most ambitious operatic venture and is the only one of Eberl's eight known theatrical works to survive in full score.[74] *Die Königin* was, however, a failure, running for only eight performances. The libretto, adapted from Wieland by Johann Schwaldopler, was singled out by the critics as the principal culprit, although the stage effects were also poorly done. Eberl's music was described as often beautiful but untheatrical.[75] Gerber says that Haydn praised the work.

Meanwhile, in March 1801 Eberl's patron Alexander I had ascended the Russian throne. In the latter part of the year Eberl returned to St. Petersburg and dedicated his only string quartets, the set of three, Op. 13, to the new emperor, receiving a diamond ring in return. Eberl was later to dedicate the Symphony in D minor, Op. 34, to Alexander, who seems to have been the only person to receive three dedications from Eberl. In December 1801 Eberl conducted three performances of *Die Schöpfung* in St. Petersburg with great success. He evidently did not find sufficient encouragement to stay in Russia, however, for in 1802 he returned to Vienna.

After the failure of *Die Königin*, Eberl seems to have dedicated himself to instrumental music with a new vigor. He finally overcame many of his previous technical limitations and went on to enjoy five years of successes as a composer that ended only with his sudden death in 1807. Eberl dedicated his first mature piano sonata, Op. 12, to Haydn; it was the first work of his to receive a wholly positive review from the *Allgemeine musi-*

*kalische Zeitung.*[76] August von Kotzebue, passing through Vienna during Carnival in 1803, reported that the two favorite chamber works at the amateur musicales were Beethoven's Quintet for piano and winds, Op. 16, and Eberl's Quartet for piano and strings, Op. 18.[77] It was just at this time that Eberl must have been composing the work that was to establish him as one of the leading symphonists of the younger generation.

On 6 January 1804, in a concert in the Jahnischer Saal, Eberl brought forth several recent works. The event received quite a bit of attention in the press. The first of two accounts in the *Allgemeine musikalische Zeitung* concerns Eberl's piano playing:

> Herr Eberl indisputably belongs to the *Starkspieler* (as they are called here) among the local virtuosi on this instrument, and stands on the same level as Madame Auer[n]hammer, Beethoven, and Wölfl, but with the reservation that, unlike these last, he does not know how to give his playing enough light and shadow.[78]

From the second review, written by the Eberl partisan who was quoted earlier, we learn that the program included the overture to *Die Königin*, the Piano concerto in E-flat major, Op. 40, the Concerto for two pianos and orchestra in B-flat major, Op. 45, and the Symphony in E-flat major, Op. 33. This critic had good words for almost everything, but it was the symphony that made him wax ecstatic:

> A big new symphony by Eberl, dedicated to Prince Lobkowitz . . . is extraordinarily successful, full of bold and new ideas. . . . After the first, beautifully worked-out but very long Allegro in E-flat comes a splendid Andante in C minor in which the wind instruments are beau-

---

[74] The extant MS score, Vienna, Österreichische Nationalbibliothek K.T. 250, was misidentified by Ewens, *Eberl*, 121, as an autograph. The call number indicates that its provenance is the former Kärntnertortheater collection. To judge from the facsimiles in White, "Eberl," it is most likely the work of a group of professional copyists, presumably a conductor's score made by the theater staff for the performances.

[75] *AMZ* III (1800–1801) cols. 785–86, 797–98; a more extensive report appears in the *Berlinische musikalische Zeitung* I (1805), No. 32, p. 128; No. 43, p. 169–70; No. 48, p. 189–90; and No. 62, p. 245–46.

[76] *AMZ* V (1802–1803) cols. 558–60. Haydn's copy of the sonata can be traced in the catalogues of his library and the inventory of his estate; see Landon, *Haydn: chronicle and works* V, 304, 228.

[77] In *Der Freymüthige*, No. 58 (12 April 1803), quoted in *TDR* II, 379–80; *TK* II, 1–2; *TF* I, 324–25.

[78] *AMZ* VI (1803–1804) col. 294.

tifully employed, and in which the passage where the cellos, clarinets, and bassoons carry the theme [m. 57ff.] makes an extraordinary effect. The finale in E-flat shows genuine originality and artistic merit. . . . The spot was most pleasing where Eberl moved from A-flat to C major by means of an enharmonic change to G-sharp [m. 401]. May this symphony soon be made generally available through print and may Herr Eberl further employ his talents in this genre![79]

From the dedication of the symphony to Lobkowitz one may infer that the prince had already enjoyed exclusive rights to the work for a period, probably six months, and that this performance was simply the first one open to the public. That suggests that the work had been completed toward the middle of 1803.

Eberl did not wait long to compose another symphony. A year after the concert just described, he gave another in the same hall on 25 January 1805. The principal novelty was the premiere of the Symphony in D minor, Op. 34:

> An entirely new symphony in D by Eberl also belongs to his most successful compositions. It begins with a short Largo in D minor, which is then interrupted by a bold, beautifully executed march in D major. There follows a very beautifully worked-out Allegro, then a beautiful, expressive Andante, and finally the whole concludes with a majestic double fugue.[80]

Meanwhile, the Symphony in E-flat major had received its most famous performance in a series of semi-professional concerts at the home of the Viennese banker von Würth on Sunday mornings. The performance of the Eberl symphony came just a week after a performance of the "Eroica," and the correspondent for the *Allgemeine musikalische Zeitung*, who had not heard Beethoven's new symphony before, found the comparison between the two very much in Eberl's

favor.[81] The exact dates of these performances cannot be established, but the likely Sundays are 13, 20, and 27 January 1805, most probably 20 January for the "Eroica" and 27 January for the Eberl symphony.[82] As was indicated earlier, by April that critic had not changed his opinion about the relative merits of the "Eroica" and the Eberl symphonies.

As Eberl's reputation spread throughout the Germanic countries, he began dealing with publishers farther afield than he had previously, particularly the Leipzig firms. The D minor symphony was published by Breitkopf & Härtel in 1805 or 1806 as Op. 34. Eberl's favorite publisher in the last two years or so of his life was Kühnel, who published ten Eberl works in all, including the Symphony in E-flat major, Op. 37, and both of the mature solo piano concertos. Fragments of the correspondence between Eberl and Kühnel survive: letters by Eberl from Vienna dated 6 November 1805 and 4 January 1806 and from Dresden dated 9 March 1806.[83]

Eberl undertook an extended concert tour in the winter and spring of 1806, taking with him the overtures, symphonies, and concertos he had been performing in Vienna. The itinerary included Prague, Berlin, Dresden, Leipzig, Weimar, Gotha, Frankfurt am Main, and Mannheim; it

---

[79] AMZ VI (1803–1804) cols. 468–70.

[80] AMZ VII (1804–1805) cols. 322–23.

[81] AMZ VII (1804–1805) cols. 321–22.

[82] The report from Vienna cited in n. 81 above mentioning the performances of the "Eroica" and Eberl's Op. 33 is dated 28 January 1805. The next contribution by this correspondent, AMZ VII (1804–1805) col. 351, is dated 17 February; it mentions the failure of a symphony by Friedrich August Kanne. Wilhelm Hitzig, "Aus den Briefen Griesingers an Breitkopf und Härtel entnommene Notizen über Beethoven," *Der Bär*, 1927, 32–33, quotes a letter from Griesinger dated 13 February 1805 that states that the "Eroica" performance was an extraordinary success, that Eberl's symphony was given the next week, and that Kanne's failure came two weeks later, presumably meaning two weeks after the Beethoven performance. As the Kanne work must have been performed after 28 January, the probable dates are 3 February for Kanne, 27 January for Eberl, and 20 January for Beethoven; some leeway has to be added because of Griesinger's ambiguity.

[83] The first letter is in Philadelphia, Historical Society of Pennsylvania, Simon Gratz collection, Case 13, Box 6. The others are in Vienna, Stadt- und Landesbibliothek; both appear in facsimile and translation in White, "Eberl," 54–57.

was a great success.[84] In Weimar Eberl was warmly received by Princess Maria Paulovna, one of the younger members of the Russian imperial family and doubtless an acquaintance from Eberl's years in St. Petersburg. The princess commissioned a piano sonata from Eberl; it was to be the Sonata in G minor, Op. 39, possibly his last completed work.

Back in Vienna, Eberl resumed his performing and composing activities. He had finished Op. 39 and had several new works under way when he contracted scarlet fever and died, after a brief illness, on 11 March 1807. Although Eberl was nearly forty-two, the reaction to his death seems to have been of the sort that one would associate more with the passing of someone younger. "The early death of an artist has rarely been so generally mourned," one paper reported.[85] This is certainly due to Eberl's late start as a composer of serious instrumental music. A report of a performance of the D minor symphony in Leipzig concluded with the comment that Eberl's style was overloaded, but that "he would certainly have recovered from these minor deficiencies and remained true to his great virtues had fate only allowed him a longer life."[86] A review of the published edition of the work echoed these sentiments and voiced the wish that Eberl had been able to acquire more experience in the genre.[87]

Eberl's two mature symphonies remained in the repertory in the German-speaking countries until at least the 1830's. The last reported performance of an Eberl symphony in Leipzig took place in 1832; the work is not further identified, but it was most likely Op. 33, the one that was more

popular there.[88] An Eberl symphony was performed at a public concert of the Gesellschaft der Musikfreunde in Vienna under the direction of Eduard von Lannoy on 8 April 1832;[89] this was undoubtedly Op. 33, as a manuscript score of the work dated 9 December 1831 survives in the Musikfreunde collection.[90] Aside from a few works falsely attributed to Mozart, Eberl's other compositions suffered the same fate as the symphonies. The appearance of a few major works in modern editions[91] and a successful recent revival of the Piano concerto in C major, Op. 32,[92] suggest that a reevaluation of Eberl's work is beginning.

How well acquainted were Eberl and Beethoven? There is no indication that they were ever close friends, but they were in contact from Beethoven's arrival in Vienna in 1792 until Eberl's death in 1807. Certainly they saw each other in the Mozart circle in the early 1790's. Eberl attended Beethoven's concert of 5 April 1803, which included in its gargantuan program a performance of Symphony No. 1 and the premiere of No. 2. An acquaintance who saw him the next day reported: "Eberl told me that in yesterday's *Akademie* Beethoven had quite disappointed the legitimate expectations of the public, that nothing was altogether worthy of a great master."[93] From all accounts the affair was disorganized and under-rehearsed (one wonders how much of the negative

---

[84] Two of the more significant reviews of concerts on this tour appear in the AMZ VIII (1805–1806) cols. 462–63 and 540–41.

[85] AMZ IX (1806–1807) col. 428.

[86] AMZ X (1807–1808) col. 494.

[87] AMZ X (1807–1808) cols. 747–50. Two other substantial reviews in the AMZ are one of the Grand duo in A major for cello and piano, Op. 26, and the Piano sonata in G minor, Op. 39, XI (1808–1809) cols. 337–44, and an unfavorable one of the Piano sonata in C major, Op. 43, XI, cols. 521–22.

[88] AMZ XXXV (1833) cols. 179. Reports of other performances of Op. 33 appear in XIII (1811) col. 830, XIX (1817) col. 355, XXV (1823) col. 786, and XXIX (1827) col. 105; a performance of Op. 34 appears in XXVI (1824) col. 486.

[89] Perger and Hirschfeld, *Geschichte der K. K. Gesellschaft der Musikfreunde in Wien* (Vienna: Gesellschaft der Musikfreunde, 1912) 291.

[90] A Wgm XIII. 5031. White, "Eberl," 8–9, wishes to see this as an autograph, which it is certainly not.

[91] The only major work of Eberl's currently available in a performing edition is the Sextet for violin, viola, cello, clarinet, horn, and piano, Op. 47, ed. Werner Genuit and Dieter Klocker (London: Musica rara, 1969). An edition of the piano sonatas is in preparation by A. Duane White.

[92] Greenville, South Carolina, 19 November 1981.

[93] Quoted from an entry in the diary of Joseph Carl Rosenbaum in H. C. Robbins Landon, *Beethoven* (Zürich: Universal Edition, 1970) 259.

reaction to Beethoven's works was due to poor performances), and Eberl's disappointment was occasioned by his high expectations of Beethoven. Eberl and Beethoven were probably both composing E-flat major symphonies at this time, works with the same key scheme that would be dedicated to the same patron. How much attention Beethoven paid to Eberl's work, or to the unfavorable comparisons made by some to his own, is conjectural (in some ways Symphony No. 4 is that shorter and—on the surface—simpler

version of the "Eroica" the critic wanted). That Eberl was impressed by the "Eroica" is evident in the homage paid to it in his Op. 34, discussed below. A final link between the two appears in the Eberl letter of 9 March 1806, in which the composer reports to Kühnel that his wife has received a parcel in Vienna and that an enclosure for "Hr. v. Beethowen" has been relayed to him. Clearly they were on speaking terms, but whether there was closer contact has yet to be determined.

## Symphonic works

Eberl's symphonies fall into two groups. The three early works all survive in autographs in the Gesellschaft der Musikfreunde. Eberl made numerous changes on these scores, particularly regarding orchestration. It may be dangerous to assume that Eberl's later compositional practice was identical to that reflected in these three scores, but it seems most unlikely that he ever composed large works in his head while on walks and wrote them down later, as a necrology would have us believe.[94]

The early symphonies were not printed in Eberl's lifetime, but they did circulate in manuscript parts produced by such Viennese copying firms as that of Johann Traeg, who advertised the three works in his catalogue of 1799.[95] Viennese copies of the Symphonies in D major and C major survive in the Florence Conservatory with attributions to Franz Christoph Neubauer. The Neubauer attributions, however, appear on title pages added later in a hand not involved in copying the

music, and in the absence of any further evidence to support them they can be discounted. More spectacularly, the Symphony in C major also appears in a manuscript in Cremona in which it is ascribed to Mozart, doubtless because of the similarity of its opening to that of the "Haffner." This manuscript served as the basis for a 1944 edition of the work as a rediscovered Mozart symphony.[96]

Stylistically the three early symphonies are all very much the work of Eberl the apprentice composer; even the Symphony in C major, the most accomplished of the three, is a naive piece. The D major symphony has an introduction that foreshadows the opening allegro.[97] The work has been singled out for its remarkably high trumpet writing, going all the way up to written $D^3$ at the end

---

[94] White, "Eberl," 61, also doubts the story.

[95] Traeg catalogue (full citation in the list of catalogue references below), 7, "Sinfonien" Nos. 1–3. The works are identifiable by their keys. The scoring as listed there includes one bassoon part for each symphony; in the surviving sources, the symphonies in D major and C major each have two and the one in G major none, though a bassoon doubling the bass might be appropriate performance practice. As this catalogue is full of such errors, no significance need be attached to the discrepancy.

[96] Discussed at length in Fisher, "C-dur Sinfonie"; the original identification of the Cremona symphony as a work of Eberl was made by H. C. Robbins Landon, "Two orchestral works wrongly attributed to Mozart," *The music review* XVII (1956) 33–34. The Cremona source lacks the bassoon II; in the printed edition, edited by Nino Negrotti (Milan: Carisch, 1944), one has been reconstructed by the editor.

[97] Marianne Danckwardt, *Die langsame Einleitung: ihre Herkunft und ihr Bau bei Haydn und Mozart*, 2 vols. (Tutzing: Hans Schneider, 1977) II, 331–32, gives part of this introduction in score. The discussion on I, 40, finds the lack of internal motivic cohesion in this introduction a flaw, but Danckwardt has overlooked the connection between the opening of the introduction and the opening of the allegro, which certainly affects this matter.

of the first-movement exposition.[98] This probably reflects inexperience on Eberl's part rather than the availability of extraordinary players, although their appearance in the Florence source suggests that these trumpet parts were negotiable. Eberl's handling of the individual instruments and of the orchestra as a whole is the most obvious way in which the three early symphonies show steady improvement. In all three, particularly in the finales of the Symphonies in D major and C major, Eberl essays contrapuntal passages, but his efforts invariably result in facile parallelism. He does learn the trick of moving his thematic material around in the orchestra, but he was not to master counterpoint until much later. Only the first movement of the Symphony in D major and the second movement of the one in C major are in the type of sonata form with a complete recapitulation; in the five remaining sonata-form movements Eberl brings back only the second theme and associated material in the tonic. From the Thematic Index one may see that the openings of the D major and G major symphonies are bland; in the C major symphony and in the two late ones, the thematic material is much more striking. The opening theme of the C major symphony, of course, is modeled on that of the "Haffner"; it is not so simple and elegant as Mozart's theme, and Eberl's treatment of it is not as accomplished, but it does help to create a movement with a great deal of superficial vigor and excitement.

The autographs of Eberl's two mature symphonies, and indeed of his mature output altogether, have disappeared. Both works were published, however, and circulated widely in Eberl's lifetime and just after.

The last two symphonies show the dimensions and scoring typical of the more ambitious late Classical symphony. The Symphony in E-flat major, Op. 33, follows the common pattern of four movements with an introduction. In the D minor symphony, Op. 34, Eberl essays a variant of this form in which a march comes between the introduction and the *Allegro agitato* that comprises the main body of the first movement. There is no minuet; this march has assumed the same role in the structure although it occurs in a different position. (Eberl tries an even more complex structure in the Piano sonata in G minor, Op. 39.)

Since the juvenile symphonies, Eberl has learned the Classical art of free motivic work as well as the stricter sort of counterpoint as it was practiced in the period. Genuine counterpoint is rare outside the finales of the late symphonies, but sections in the two concluding movements are rigorously imitative. (Eberl's interest in counterpoint also surfaces in the letter to Kühnel of 6 November 1805, in which Eberl places an order for a copy of Marpurg's *Abhandlung von der Fuge*.)

Eberl's harmonic language has expanded considerably since the early symphonies. In the juvenile works, the most striking spot harmonically was a somewhat disruptive shift to the Neapolitan in the recapitulation of the first movement of the Symphony in D major. In the late symphonies the harmony not only ranges more widely but forms a more consistent and coherent overall structure. Eberl frequently reserves his most striking harmonic effects for places other than his development sections. This is in contrast to the practice of Haydn and, to some degree, Beethoven, but like Mozart's approach, although Eberl's use of colorful chords or modulations is freer than is that of the older composers. Ewens wishes to see Eberl's harmonic language as his contribution to the rise of musical Romanticism.[99] This view has merit in that Eberl's influence on the music of the next generation probably lay in his spreading of the richer harmonic vocabulary of the progressive

---

[98] Cited in J. Murray Barbour, *Trumpets, horns, and music* (East Lansing: Michigan State University Press, 1964) 132, apparently without regard to Eberl's age or lack of experience as a composer.

[99] Ewens, *Eberl*, 103–07, discusses "Eberl als Harmoniker und Romantiker."

composers of his day. On the other hand, the underlying harmonic structures in most of Eberl's work, including the symphonies, are still those of Classicism, with the more colorful elements largely serving to embellish the design. The Symphony in D minor, Op. 34, and the Piano Sonata in G minor, Op. 39, may show Eberl moving in a new direction at the end of his career. Eberl's style in general, though, is best understood in the light of its Classical antecedents.

Certainly Eberl's handling of sonata form does not greatly suggest Romanticism. The first and last movements of both late symphonies are in sonata form, but only the first movement of the Symphony in E-flat major, Op. 33, has a full recapitulation. The three remaining sonata movements only recapitulate the second theme and some of the following material. The first themes of these movements do not disappear altogether after the development section, as Eberl likes to bring the opening motif of an exposition back at some point in the second-theme or closing material, and he provides an extended coda based in part on the opening idea in the first movement of the Symphony in D minor, Op. 34. In all three movements, however, Eberl has foregone the climax at the moment of recapitulation of the opening theme that constitutes the most memorable spot in many sonata movements by Haydn, Mozart, and Beethoven. Reicha does refer to the partial recapitulation as an alternative in the discussion of sonata form in the *Traité de haute composition musicale* (treated at some length in the section on that composer), but his preference is for a complete recapitulation with enough recomposition to allow one to have a return of the opening theme in the tonic without letting the last part of the movement be a mechanical repetition of material previously heard. The partial recapitulation seems a less satisfactory approach.

By coincidence the Symphony in E-flat major, Op. 33, has the same key and movement scheme as the "Eroica." The Eberl work that is most closely related to the "Eroica," however, is the Symphony in D minor, Op. 34. Although this work was performed publicly several months before Beethoven's symphony, as noted earlier, the "Eroica" was probably first performed privately about the middle of 1804, well in advance of the premiere of Eberl's work in January 1805. As a member of the Lobkowitz circle, Eberl would undoubtedly have had a chance to become acquainted with the new symphony of which the prince was so proud. That Eberl did so cannot be doubted. In the triple-meter first movement of Eberl's work a new theme in a key a half step above the tonic, E-flat major, appears late in the development section and then returns in the tonic in the recapitulation. Although Eberl's procedure has considerably less impact than Beethoven's introduction of a new theme in E minor into a movement in E-flat major, Op. 33, the resemblance is unmistakable. In the introduction to the Symphony in D minor, Op. 34, Eberl also makes use of E-flat major, thus setting up a long-range relationship between two keys a semitone apart, an advanced procedure for 1804. There are ways in which this symphony reminds one of late more than middle Beethoven, in fact; the insertion of the march between the introduction and first allegro and the replacement of the development section of the finale with a fugue on a new theme (to which the opening theme is later added) show a breakdown in the concept of the movement as a self-contained entity (the Op. 39 piano sonata also shows such tendencies). Eberl was clearly thinking along very radical lines; whether he carried out his plans as well as he thought them up is unfortunately doubtful.

# Symphony in E-flat major, Op. 33

As was indicated earlier, this work was probably finished about the middle of 1803; possibly it had been begun the preceding year, though it is not likely to have been finished so far in advance of its first public performance. Eberl's letter to Kühnel of 4 January 1806 indicates that Kühnel was using the autograph score as the basis for the edition. The letter of 6 November 1805 shows Eberl declining to read some proofs; although this may not have referred to this work, it may be assumed that Eberl did not do so for any of the works published by Kühnel. The edition appeared about the end of 1806.[100] No textual studies have been made to see if there is an independent manuscript source tradition for the piece, but the copy of the score in the Gesellschaft der Musikfreunde or the set of parts in the former Lobkowitz collection[101] may not be dependent on the printed edition.

The first movement is an *Allegro con fuoco e vivace* with a brief introduction, *Andante sostenuto*. Disregarding the introductions (Beethoven's is considerably longer) this movement is almost precisely as long as the first movement of Beethoven's Symphony No. 2, 323 measures to Beethoven's 327. Eberl writes more extended closing sections in the exposition and recapitulation but Beethoven writes a longer development, roughly eighty measures to Eberl's fifty. Eberl's development is, however, more intense and more Classical in its harmonic structure, placing greater emphasis on tonalities to the sharp side of the tonic than Beethoven's. Both movements have codas of about fifty measures.

Eberl was fond of march movements in his larger instrumental works. Besides the C minor second movement of the Symphony in E-flat ma-

jor, he composed a march second movement in E-flat major for the Concerto for two pianos in B-flat major, Op. 45, and, of course, a march movement in the Symphony in D minor, Op. 34. The similarity in key between the present *Andante con moto* and the slow movement of the "Eroica" is undoubtedly coincidental; Eberl's march is a jaunty little "Hungarian" piece. As the *Menuetto* that follows is a nearly through-composed piece with two trios, the two inner movements of the symphony have nearly the same weight.

The very opening of Eberl's finale, *Allegro assai*, and the returns of the initial motif in different contrapuntal guises throughout the exposition reveal that the model for the movement was the finale of Mozart's "Jupiter" symphony, K. 551. On paper Eberl's movement is slightly longer (disregarding Mozart's instructions to repeat the development and recapitulation), 461 measures to Mozart's 424 (Eberl's quarter note equals Mozart's half, so the measures have the same sounding length). This finale, however, does not rise to the level of Mozart's; it is neither so complex contrapuntally nor so tightly organized. The contrapuntal passages alternate with homophonic ones employing thematic ideas that never join in the polyphony (one idea, first appearing at m. 49, may be a reminiscence of the first movement). Eberl's coda, although harmonically striking, makes no attempt to rival Mozart's; the contrapuntal material vanishes almost entirely. The proportions of the sections within the movement reveal a very different approach. Eberl's finale is longer because of its longer closing area in the exposition and its longer development, roughly ninety measures to sixty. His recapitulation, however, encompasses only some seventy measures of second-theme and closing material while Mozart's is complete and nearly twice as long. Nearly half Mozart's finale is still to come after the beginning

---

[100] The plate No. is 501; Deutsch, *Musikverlags Nummern*, 13–14, assigns it to 1806–1807.

[101] CS Pnm X. g. c. 25.

of the recapitulation, compared to only a third of Eberl's. As Eberl's movement is monothematic, unlike Mozart's, his elimination of the first theme and transition is sensible enough (though not as elegant as the telescoping one encounters in such places as the first movements of Haydn's Symphony No. 100 or Mozart's "Prague" symphony, K. 504) and the end of the recapitulation is replaced by the coda. The result is to give the end of the movement less weight in the overall structure, which might not be the best state of affairs in a finale.

As some of the contemporary criticism hints and as Hermann Kretzschmar noted,[102] Eberl's Achilles heel as a composer was probably melody and thematic construction. A comparison of some passages from the first movement of the Symphony in E-flat major with their equivalents in Beethoven's Symphony No. 1, Op. 21 (1800), and overture to *Die Geschöpfe des Prometheus* (1800/1801) will illustrate this.

All three movements have brief introductions leading to allegros in cut time. The opening paragraphs of the allegros all begin with a phrase starting on the tonic that is repeated a tone higher, after which a third phrase leads to a tutti counterstatement of the opening. The repetition of the opening phrase of a theme a tone higher is a common stereotype, particularly with Beethoven, who varied the pattern in a number of ways.[103] The *Prometheus* overture gives the stereotype in straightforward form (m. 17ff.) with phrases of four, four, and five measures. The third phrase starts melodically on the third degree, with tonic harmony, and ends with an acceleration of the harmonic rhythm to quarter notes just before the

half cadence in measure 28. Symphony No. 1 (m. 13ff.) expands the structure by extending the first two phrases to six measures each and the third phrase to nine. The third phrase begins melodically on the leading tone, with dominant harmony, and ascends the dominant seventh chord in two-measure steps that represent an acceleration of the opening six-measure units. The harmony pauses on the dominant seventh for six measures, building up a tension that Beethoven increases when he shifts gears in measure 31 to *fortissimo* chords on the beat, driving to an elision at the big downbeat in measure 33. Beethoven has not altered any fundamental aspect of the stereotype, but he has created a much more powerful and expressive passage by avoiding four-measure construction and by shaping the whole to reach a climax in measure 33. Eberl's theme (m. 19ff.) more closely resembles that of the overture, beginning with two four-measure phrases and proceeding melodically up to the third degree, with tonic harmony, at the beginning of the third phrase. The third phrase accelerates the melodic and harmonic motion, rushing up to a surprising G-flat in measure 30. Eberl drives to a deceptive cadence in measure 36 and then to a tonic cadence at the elision in measure 40. This structure is imaginative and ambitious, and it keeps up the forward motion, but it lacks the sweep and the cumulation of tension that the one in Beethoven's symphony achieves. Eberl has sacrificed a great deal on the phrase and higher levels to achieve the excitement he wants on the levels of the motif and subphrase.

In all three movements the second theme group begins with an eight-measure unit scored primarily for the winds, after which the strings enter. In the *Prometheus* overture (m. 49ff.) the eight measures comprise an antecedent-consequent phrase pair. Eberl (m. 74ff.) also assays a pair of complementary phrases—a rather banal passage, especially as both phrases end with the same half cadence. Again the Beethoven symphony (m. 53ff.) shows the most interesting

---

[102] Kretzschmar, *Führer*, 208–09.

[103] See James Webster, "Traditional elements in Beethoven's middle-period string quartets," *Beethoven, performers, and critics: the international Beethoven congress, Detroit, 1977* (Detroit: Wayne State University Press, 1980) 105–11, and the literature cited in n. 5. A Haydn example not mentioned by Webster occurs at the beginning of the finale of the Piano sonata in E-flat major, Hob. XVI:52.

structure, a single eight-measure unit that reveals a much greater sense of forward motion. Beethoven's thematic construction shows occasional lapses into the trivial, but on the whole he is decidedly better than Eberl in this regard.

Considering the symphony as a whole, one can see what the critic saw in it to prefer it to the "Eroica" and yet one can see equally well why Beethoven's symphony prevailed in the repertory while this one was forgotten. "Light, clarity, and unity" were the principles invoked by the anonymous critic. This work manifests all three, while the "Eroica" was and is difficult to grasp at first. Once this was understood the work was widely and enthusiastically accepted. What determined its fate ultimately, though, was the skill with which it was constructed. The "Eroica" could survive repeated hearings better than Eberl's Symphony in E-flat major even if a first reaction might have favored the Eberl. Still, although there is no doubt as to who was the better composer, it may be questioned whether Eberl's music deserves the complete obscurity that is its current fate.

## Editorial method

This score was prepared from the printed edition of the parts by Kühnel. Editorial additions of notes, accidentals, dynamics, and groups of three or more staccato marks appear in brackets; added ties and slurs are indicated with a vertical slash through them. Inconsistencies in parallel passages have on occasion been altered to bring parts into conformity with one another. Inconsistencies in the use of *fz*, *sf*, *f*, and *ff* and inconsistencies between the use of dots and strokes for staccato have been altered tacitly.

In the printed parts the three occurrences of the main section of the third movement are almost identical, indicating that the section must have been written out only once in the autograph, which served as engraver's copy for the edition. This score returns to the probable format of the autograph by giving the main section only once.

Although Kühnel's edition is a careful one by the standards of the period, some textual problems remain. One particularly troublesome one concerns the rhythm in measures 94–101 and 254–61 of the first movement. The source has ties over the bar lines in measures 94–95, ob I, 254–55, fl I and II, ob I and II, and 260–61, fl II, but as the other parts with the same figure lack ties, they have been omitted in this score.

## Acknowledgments

My initial scholarly work on the symphonies of Beethoven's contemporaries and of Eberl in particular was done several years ago under the direction of John Hill; I wish to thank him both for his assistance then and for his making his research material available once more for the preparation of this volume. Duane White's encouragement has also been most welcome. Sterling Murray, Richard Claypool, and Gertraut Haberkamp all kindly provided information for the Witt Thematic Index. Jan LaRue's "Identifier Catalogue of the Eighteenth-Century Symphony" was most helpful in preparing the thematic indexes. I would like especially to thank the numerous librarians who answered my inquiries or served as my hosts while I was researching the works of all three composers. Barry Brook and Barbara Heyman assisted in numerous ways with the work on this volume, and Leo Balk, Ann Callaway, David Froom, and Matthew Greenbaum at Garland were indispensable. Douglas Johnson kindly read a draft of this introduction, offering helpful crit-

icism on a number of points. Any remaining flaws are, of course, my responsibility.

Stephen C. Fisher
Philadelphia, Pennsylvania
August 1983

# Bibliography

[Unsigned necrology]. *Allgemeine musikalische Zeitung* IX (1806/1807) cols. 423–30.

Eitner, Robert. *Biographisch-bibliographisches Quellen-Lexikon der Musiker und Musikgelehrten.* 11 vols. Leipzig: Breitkopf & Härtel, 1898–1904. III, 300–02, 306.

Ewens, Franz Joseph. *Anton Eberl: ein Beitrag zur Musikgeschichte in Wien um 1800.* Dresden: Limpert, 1927.

Fisher, Stephen C. "Die C-dur Sinfonie KV Anh. C 11.14: ein Jugendwerk Anton Eberls," *Mitteilungen der internationalen Stiftung Mozarteum* [forthcoming].

Gerber, Ernst Ludwig. *Neues historisch-biographisches Lexikon der Tonkünstler.* 4 vols. Leipzig: Kühnel, 1812–1814. II, cols. 3–7.

Haas, Robert. "Anton Eberl," *Mozart-Jahrbuch 1951*, 123–30.

Kretzschmar, Hermann. *Führer durch den Concertsaal, I. Abtheilung: Sinfonie und Suite, I. Band.* Leipzig: Breitkopf & Härtel, 1898. 208–10.

Landon, H. C. Robbins. "Two orchestral works wrongly attributed to Mozart," *The music review* XVII (1956) 29–34.

Mies, Paul. "Eberl," in "Orchestral music of Beethoven's contemporaries," *The age of Beethoven, 1790–1830.* The new Oxford history of music VIII, ed. Gerald Abraham. London: Oxford University Press, 1982. 175–76.

White, A. Duane. "Eberl, Anton," *The new Grove dictionary of music and musicians*, ed. Stanley Sadie. 20 vols. London: Macmillan, 1980. V, 812–13.

———. "The piano works of Anton Eberl (1765–1807)." Ph.D. dissertation, University of Wisconsin, 1971. University Microfilm 71-20,699.

# Thematic Index: Witt

*I wish to thank Jan LaRue and Sterling Murray for generously placing their research materials at my disposal during the initial stages of this investigation.*

**Total:** 23 symphonies

**Numbering:** Nos. 1–9 follow the numbering of the André editions; the remaining works have been assigned numbers arbitrarily pending fuller source and stylistic investigation. An asterisk indicates the score published in this volume.

**Instrumentation:** Given according to the list of "Abbreviations for musical instruments."

**Date:** Based on external evidence only. It is likely that Nos. 10–23 are all earlier than Nos. 1 and 2 and that the remainder of the nine published works appeared in the order of composition, but this cannot be stated with certainty. For a more extended discussion, see the Introduction.

**Sources:** Unless otherwise indicated, sources are parts. Manuscript sources are indicated by *RISM* library sigla (see list) and shelf mark. Printed sources are listed by city, publisher, and plate number; where it could be established that an exemplar is complete, the abbreviation "cmpl." appears in parentheses after the library siglum.

**Modern scores:** Editor and publisher are identified.

**Orchestral materials:** Editor and publisher or rental library are identified.

**Recordings:** Orchestra, conductor, record company, and catalogue number are given.

## 1 Symphony No. 1 in B-flat major

I. Adagio—Allegro vivace   II. Adagio
III. Menuetto—Trio   IV. Finale: Allegro

| | |
|---|---|
| *Instr.:* | 2 vl, vla, b, fl, 2 ob, 2 cl, 2 fag, 2 cor, 2 tr, timp |
| *Date:* | First ed. 1803/1804 |
| *Cat. Ref.:* | Jerkowitz |
| *Sources:* | Offenbach: André (*Sinfonie à grand orchestre*) Pl. No. 1886; **GB** Lbm, **NL** At |
| | *Ibid.*, Pl. No. 1887 (also 289); **US** BETm (cmpl.), **US** NYp (cmpl.) |
| *Orch. Mat.:* | Edwin A. Fleisher Collection, Free Library of Philadelphia, Philadelphia, PA 19103 |

## *2 Symphony No. 2 in D major

I. Grave—Allegro non tanto   II. Adagio
III. Menuetto—Trio   IV. Allegro non tanto

| | |
|---|---|
| *Instr.:* | 2 vl, vla, b, fl, 2 ob, 2 fag, 2 cor, 2 tr, timp |
| *Date:* | First ed. 1803/1804 |
| *Cat. Ref.:* | Göttweig, Witt 2 (entry 2955) |
| *Sources:* | Offenbach: André (*Sinfonie à grand orchestre*) Pl. No. 1887; **D-brd** Mbs (cmpl.), **NL** At, **US** BETm (cmpl.), **US** Wc (cmpl.) |

| | |
|---|---|
| *Mod. Score:* | Ed. by Stephen C. Fisher, Garland, 1983 (B IX 1) |
| *Orch. Mat.:* | Edwin A. Fleisher Collection, Free Library of Philadelphia, Philadelphia, PA 19103 |

## 3 Symphony No. 3 in F major

I. Adagio—Allegro assai   II. Andante
III. Menuetto—Trio   IV. Finale

| | |
|---|---|
| *Instr.:* | 2 vl, vla, b, 2 fl, 2 ob, 2 cl, 2 fag, 2 cor, 2 tr, timp |
| *Date:* | First ed. 1806 |
| *Sources:* | Offenbach: André (*Sinfonie à grand orchestre*) Pl. No. 2354; **B** Bc, **CH** Zz (cmpl.), **D-ddr** SWl, **NL** At, **US** BETm (cmpl.), **US** NYp (cmpl.) |

## 4 Symphony No. 4 in E-flat major

*mezza voce*

I. Adagio sostenuto—Allegro vivace
II. Adagio ma un poco andante   III. Menuetto: Allegro—Trio
IV. Finale: Allegro molto

| | |
|---|---|
| *Instr.:* | 2 vl, vla, b, 2 fl, 2 ob, 2 cl, 2 fag, 2 cor, 2 tr, timp |
| *Date:* | First ed. 1806 |
| *Sources:* | Offenbach: André (*Sinfonie à grand orchestre*) Pl. No. |

2367; **B** Bc, **CH** Zz (cmpl.), **D-brd** Mbs (cmpl.), **NL** At, **US** BETm (cmpl.), **US** NYp (cmpl.), **US** Wc (cmpl.)

*Sources:* Offenbach: André (*Grande sinfonie*) Pl. No. 3014; **D-brd** Mbs (cmpl.), **NL** At, **US** BETm (cmpl.), **US** NYp (cmpl.), **US** Wc (cmpl.)

## 5 Symphony No. 5 in D major

I. Adagio—Allegro  II. Andante grazioso
III. Minuetto: Allegro—Trio  IV. Finale: Allegro

*Instr.:* 2 vl, vla, b, 2 fl, 2 ob, 2 cl, 2 fag, 2 cor, 2 tr, timp

*Date:* First ed. 1808

*Sources:* Offenbach: André (*Grand sinfonie*) Pl. No. 2622; **D-brd** DO, **GB** Lbm (cmpl.), **US** BETm (cmpl.), **US** Wc (cmpl.)
*Ibid.*, Pl. No. 4311; **US** NYp (cmpl.)

## 6 Symphony No. 6 in A minor, "Sinfonie turque"

I. Adagio—Allegro molto  II. Adagio
III. Minuetto: Allegretto—Trio  IV. Finale: Allegro

*Instr.:* 2 vl, vla, b, 2 fl, 2 ob, 2 cl, 2 fag, 4 cor, 2 tr, timp, g.c., tamb, tri, cym

*Date:* First ed. 1808

*Sources:* Offenbach: André (*Sinfonie turque*) Pl. No. 2639; **B** Bc, **D-brd** DO (cmpl.), **US** BETm (cmpl.)

## 7 Symphony No. 7 in C major

I. Adagio—Allegro vivace assai
II. Adagio cantabile ma un poco andante
III. Minuetto: Allegro—Trio  IV. Allegro

*Instr.:* 2 vl, vla, b, guitar, 2 fl, 2 ob, 2 fag, 2 cor, 2 tr, timp

*Date:* First ed. 1810/1811

*Sources:* Offenbach: André (*Grande sinfonie*) Pl. No. 3013; **B** Bc, **GB** Lbm, **US** BETm (2 ex.)

## 8 Symphony No. 8 in E major

I. Adagio—Allegro vivace  II. Andante
III. Minuetto: Allegro molto assai—Trio
IV. Finale: Allegro non tanto

*Instr.:* 2 vl, vla, b, 2 fl, 2 ob, 2 cl, 2 fag, 2 cor, 2 tr, timp

*Date:* First ed. 1810/1811

## 9 Symphony No. 9 in D minor

I. Adagio—Allegro vivace  II. Adagio cantabile
III. Minuetto: Più allegro—Trio  IV. Finale: Allegro

*Instr.:* 2 vl, vla, b, 2 fl, 2 ob, 2 cl, 2 fag, 2 cor, 2 tr, timp

*Date:* First ed. *ca.* 1816

*Sources:* Offenbach: André (*Grande sinfonie*) Pl. No. 3719; **D-ddr** RUh, **US** BETm (cmpl.), **US** NYp (cmpl.), **US** Wc (cmpl.)

## 10 Symphony in C major

I. Allegro maestoso  II. Adagio  III. Menuetto: Allegro
IV. Finale: Allegro

*Instr.:* 2 vl, vla, b, fl, 2 ob, 2 fag, 2 cor

*Date:* **D-brd** HR copied 1790

*Sources:* **D-brd** HR III 4½ 2° 661
**D-brd** WD 956

## 11 Symphony in D major

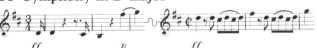

I. Adagio maestoso—Allegro assai  II. Andante non tanto
III. Menuetto: Maestoso—Trio I—Trio II  IV. Allegro spiritoso

*Instr.:* 2 vl, vla, b, 2 fl, 2 ob, 2 fag, 2 cor, 2 tr, timp

*Date:* **D-brd** HR copied 1790

*Cat. Ref.:* Thurn und Taxis, Witt 2

*Sources:* **D-brd** HR III 4½ 2° 662
**D-brd** Mbs Mus. Ms. 6857

## 12 Symphony in B-flat major

I. Largo—Allegro molto  II. Andante più allegro
III. Menuetto: Allegro—Trio  IV. Allegretto più tosto

*Instr.:* 2 vl, vla, b, fl, 2 ob, 2 fag, 2 cor

*Date:* Parts in **D-brd** HR copied 1790

*Cat. Ref.:* Thurn und Taxis, Witt 8

*Sources:* **D-brd** HR III 4½ 2° 660 ("Friderico Witt")
**D-brd** HR III 4½ 4° 627 (score; ascribed to "Feldmajer" by later hand)

**D-brd** Rtt Witt 5 ("Fr. Witt"; includes 2 tr, timp)
**D-brd** WD 957 ("Friederico Witt")

| | |
|---|---|
| *Mod. Score:* | Ed. by Fritz Zobeley, Wiesbaden: Breitkopf & Härtel, 1968 (after **D-brd** WD) |
| *Orch. Mat.:* | As above |

## 13 Symphony in C minor

I. Adagio—Allegro   II. Adagio cantabile
III. Menuetto: Allegro   IV. Finale: Allegro

| | |
|---|---|
| *Instr.:* | 2 vl, vla, b, fl, 2 ob, 2 fag, 2 cor |
| *Date:* | **D-brd** HR copied 1790 |
| *Cat. Ref.:* | Thurn und Taxis, Witt 4 |
| *Sources:* | **D-brd** HR III 4½ 2° 665 (lacks opening Adagio) |
| | **D-brd** Rtt Witt 6 |

## 14 Symphony in C major, "Jena"

I. Adagio—Allegro vivace   II. Adagio cantabile
III. Menuetto: Maestoso—Trio   IV. Finale: Allegro

| | |
|---|---|
| *Instr.:* | 2 vl, vla, b, fl, 2 ob, 2 fag, 2 cor, 2 tr, timp |
| *Date:* | 1792 or later; probably before 1800 |
| *Cat. Ref.:* | Göttweig, Witt 1 (entry 2954) |
| *Sources:* | **A** GÖ Witt 1 ("Witt") |
| | **D-ddr** Ju Ms. Conc. Acad. 69 ("P.F.W."; "Louis van Beethoven"; lacks first measure) |
| | **D-ddr** RUh ("Witt"; lacks first measure; lacks fag II, b) |
| *Mod. Score:* | Ed. by Fritz Stein, Leipzig: Breitkopf & Härtel, 1911 (after source in **D-ddr** Ju); attributed to Beethoven |
| *Orch. Mat.:* | As above |
| *Recordings:* | Saxon State Orchestra, Franz Konwitschny, DG LPE 17077 (as Beethoven); Moscow Radio Symphony Orchestra, Ruben Vartanyan, Melodiya C 01611 (as Beethoven); Munich Philharmonic Orchestra, Marc Andreae, BASF DC 223302 |

## 15 Symphony in E-flat major

I. Adagio—Allegro molto   II. Adagio non tanto
III. Menuet: Fresco   IV. Finale: Allegro

| | |
|---|---|
| *Instr.:* | 2 vl, vla, b, fl, 2 ob, 2 fag, 2 cor |
| *Date:* | **D-brd** HR copied 4 May 1793 |
| *Sources:* | **D-brd** HR III 4½ 2° 659 |
| | **D-ddr** SWl (with 2 tr, timp) |

## 16 Symphony in A major

I. Adagio—Allegro vivace   II. Menuetto: Allegro—Trio
III. Andante   IV. Allegretto

| | |
|---|---|
| *Instr.:* | 2 vl, vla, b, fl, 2 ob, 2 fag, 2 cor |
| *Date:* | Probably before 1800 |
| *Cat. Ref.:* | Thurn und Taxis, Witt 5 |
| *Sources:* | **D-brd** Rtt Witt 3 |
| | **D-ddr** Ju Ms. Conc. Acad. 68 |
| *Mod. Score:* | Ed. by Gerhard Staar, Leipzig: Breitkopf & Härtel, 1963 (based on **D-ddr** Ju); reprinted Miami: Edwin F. Kalmus, n.d. |
| *Orch. Mat.:* | As above |
| *Recording:* | Munich Philharmonic Orchestra, Marc Andreae, BASF DC 223302 |

## 17 Symphony in G major

I. Adagio—Allegro assai   II. Andante con variazioni
III. Menuetto: Allegretto   IV. Allegro

| | |
|---|---|
| *Instr.:* | 2 vl, vla, b, fl, 2 ob, 2 fag, 2 cor |
| *Date:* | Probably before 1800 |
| *Cat. Ref.:* | Thurn und Taxis, Witt 6 |
| *Source:* | **D-brd** Rtt Witt 1 |

## 18 Symphony in F major

I. Allegro molto   II. Adagio cantabile
III. Menuetto: Allegro   IV. Finale: Allegro

| | |
|---|---|
| *Instr.:* | 2 vl, vla, b, fl, 2 ob, 2 fag, 2 cor |
| *Date:* | Probably before 1800 |
| *Cat. Ref.:* | Thurn und Taxis, Witt 7 |
| *Source:* | **D-brd** Rtt Witt 4 |

## 19 Symphony in C major

I. Adagio—Allegro moderato   II. Andante   III. Menuetto
IV. Rondo: Allegretto

| | |
|---|---|
| *Instr.:* | 2 vl, vla, b, 2 ob, 2 fag, 2 cor |
| *Date:* | Probably before 1800 |
| *Source:* | **D-brd** Mbs Mus. Ms. 6856 |

## 20 Symphony in D major

I. Adagio—Allegro   II. Andante   III. Menuetto
IV.  Allegro moderato

| | |
|---|---|
| *Instr.:* | 2 vl, vla, b, 2 fl, 2 ob, 2 cor |
| *Date:* | Probably before 1800 |
| *Source:* | **D-brd** Mbs Mus. Ms. 6855 (fragmentary; only 2 vl, vla) |

## 21  Symphony in D major

I. Allegro molto   II. Andante   III. Menuetto   IV. Finale: Allegro

| | |
|---|---|
| *Instr.:* | 2 vl, vla, b, 2 ob, 2 cor |
| *Date:* | Probably before 1800 |
| *Source:* | **D-brd** Mbs Mus. Ms. 6858 |

## 22  Symphony in E-flat major

I. Allegro   II. Andante   III. Minuetto—Trio   IV. Presto

| | |
|---|---|
| *Instr.:* | 2 vl, vla, b, fl, 2 ob, 2 fag, 2 cor |
| *Date:* | Probably before 1800 |
| *Cat. Ref.:* | Thurn und Taxis, Witt 1 |
| *Source:* | **D-brd** WD 958 |

## 23  Symphony in D major

I. Allegro spiritoso

| | |
|---|---|
| *Instr.:* | 2 vl, vla, b, fl, 2 ob, 2 fag, 2 cor, 2 tr, timp |
| *Date:* | Probably before 1800 |
| *Cat. Ref.:* | Thurn und Taxis, Witt 3 |
| *Source:* | **D-brd** Rtt Witt 2 |

# Thematic Index: Eberl

*The first-movement incipits in the list below have been cross-checked for possibilities of conflicting attribution in "An Identifier Catalogue of the Eighteenth-Century Symphony" by Jan LaRue.*

**Total:** 5 symphonies

**Numbering:** As given in the thematic catalogue in A. Duane White, "The piano works of Anton Eberl (1765–1807)," Ph.D. dissertation, University of Wisconsin, 1971. The symphonies are given in chronological order. An asterisk indicates the score published in this volume; w.o.n. before a number signifies "without opus number."

**Instrumentation:** Given according to the list of "Abbreviations for musical instruments."

**Date:** For the first three symphonies, taken from the autographs; for the last two, probable dates of completion as discussed in the introduction

**Sources:** Unless otherwise indicated, sources are parts. Manuscript sources are indicated by *RISM* library sigla (see list); provenance (in parentheses); shelf mark. Printed sources are listed by city, publisher, and *RISM* A/I number (the exemplars listed have been ascertained to be complete; the others are given in *RISM*).

| | |
|---|---|
| *Mod. Score:* | Ed. by Nino Negrotti, Milan: Carisch, 1944 (as Mozart; out of print) |
| *Orch. Mat.:* | Ed. by Nino Negrotti, Milan: Carisch, 1944 (see above; copy in Edwin A. Fleisher Collection, Free Library of Philadelphia, Philadelphia, PA 19103) |

## w.o.n.5  Symphony in D major

I. Maestoso—Allegro assai   II. Andantino   III. Menuetto: Allegretto
IV. Allegro non troppo

| | |
|---|---|
| *Instr.:* | 2 vl, vla, b, 2 ob, 2 fag, 2 cor, 2 tr, timp |
| *Date:* | 10 September 1783 |
| *Cat. Ref.:* | Traeg 1799, p. 7, No. 63 |
| *Sources:* | **A** Wgm XIII. 18640 (autograph score) |
| | **I** Fc D-V-79 (as Neubauer) |

## w.o.n.6  Symphony in G major

I. Allegro vivace   II. Andantino   III. Menuetto: Allegretto
IV. Finale: Presto

| | |
|---|---|
| *Instr.:* | 2 vl, vla, b, 2 ob, 2 cor |
| *Date:* | 9 January 1784 |
| *Cat. Ref.:* | Traeg 1799, p. 7, No. 61 |
| *Source:* | **A** Wgm XIII. 18642 (autograph score) |

## w.o.n.7  Symphony in C major

I. Allegro con brio   II. Andante grazioso   III. Finale: Allegro assai

| | |
|---|---|
| *Instr.:* | 2 vl, vla, b, fl, 2 ob, 2 fag, 2 cor, 2 tr, timp |
| *Date:* | 25 June 1785 |
| *Cat. Ref.:* | Traeg 1799, p. 7, No. 62 |
| *Sources:* | **A** Wgm XIII. 18641 (autograph score) |
| | **I** CR (Pia istituzione musicale) (as Mozart; lacks fag II) |
| | **I** Fc D-V-79 (as Neubauer) |

## *Op. 33  Symphony in E-flat major

I. Andante sostenuto—Allegro con fuoco e vivace
II. Andante con moto   III. Menuetto: Allegro vivace
IV. Finale: Allegro assai

| | |
|---|---|
| *Instr.:* | 2 vl, vla, b, 2 fl, 2 ob, 2 cl, 2 fag, 2 cor, 2 tr, timp |
| *Date:* | Probably 1803 |
| *Sources:* | Leipzig: Kühnel [ca. 1806] (*Simphonie . . . Oe. XXXIII*). *RISM* e-101: **CH** Bu, **US** BETm, **US** Wc |
| | **A** Wgm XIII.5031 (score) |
| | **CS** Pnm (Lobkowitz) X.g.c.25 |
| | **D-brd** Sl Ms. XVII, 158 |
| *Mod. Score:* | Ed. by Barbara Coeyman and Stephen C. Fisher, Garland, 1983 (B IX 4) |

## Op. 34  Symphony in D minor

I. Andante maestoso e sostenuto—Tempo di marcia—Allegro agitato
II. Andante con moto   III. Finale: Vivace assai

| | |
|---|---|
| *Instr.:* | 2 vl, vla, b, 2 fl, 2 ob, 2 cl, 2 fag, 2 cor, 2 tr, timp |
| *Date:* | 1804/1805 |
| *Sources:* | Leipzig: Breitkopf [ca. 1805/1806] (*Sinfonie à grand orchestre*). *RISM* e-102: **CH** Zz, **US** Wc |
| | **D-brd** DO Mus. Ms. 402 |
| | **D-ddr** SWl Mus. 1748/2 |

# Abbreviations for musical instruments

| | | | | |
|---|---|---|---|---|
| vl | violino | cor | corno |
| vla | viola | tr | tromba |
| b | basso (violoncello e basso) | timp | timpani |
| fl | flauto | g.c. | gran cassa (bass drum) |
| ob | oboe | tamb | tambourine |
| cl | clarinetto | tri | triangolo |
| fag | fagotto (bassoon) | cym | cymbals |

# Catalogue references

*Further description of the following catalogues (except the nonthematic Traeg catalogue) can be found in Barry S. Brook, Thematic catalogues in music: an annotated bibliography (New York: Pendragon Press, 1972); references thereto are given in brackets.*

**Göttweig** "Katalogus Operum Musicalium in choro musicali Monasterii O.S.P.B. Gottwicensis R.R.D.D. Altmanno Abbate per R.D. Henricus Wondratsch p.t. chori regentem, conscriptus. Anno MDCCCXXX Tom. 1" **A** GÖ; facsimile edition with commentary by Friedrich W. Riedel as *Der Göttweiger thematische Katalog von 1830*, 2 vols. (Munich-Salzburg: Katzbichler, 1979) [Brook No. 471]

**Jerkowitz** "Thematisches Verzeichniss der dem Unterzeichneten angehörenden Musikalien. Jos. Jerkowitz.

Schasslowitz den 1. Juli 1832" **D-brd** Mbs [Brook No. 632]

**Thurn und Taxis** "Catalogus sämtlicher Hochfürstl. Thurn und Taxisch. Sinphonien" **D-brd** Rtt [Brook no. 1032]

**Traeg** *Verzeichniss alter und neuer Musikalien sowohl geschriebener als gestochener Musikalien, welche in der Kunst- und Musikalienhandlung des Johann Traeg . . . zu haben sind* (Vienna: Traeg, 1799; reprint, ed. Alexander Weinmann, Vienna: Universal Edition, 1973) [nonthematic]

# Library sigla

## A  AUSTRIA

GÖ        Göttweig, Benediktinerstift Göttweig, Musikarchiv
Wgm       Vienna, Gesellschaft der Musikfreunde

## B  BELGIUM

Bc        Brussels, Conservatoire Royal de Musique, Bibliothèque

## CH  SWITZERLAND

Bu        Basel, Öffentliche Bibliothek der Universität, Musiksammlung
Zz        Zurich, Zentralbibliothek, Kantons-, Stadt- und Universitätsbibliothek (und Bibliothek der Allgemeinen Musikgesellschaft)

## CS CZECHOSLOVAKIA

Pnm      Prague, Národní muzeum, hudební oddělení

## D-brd FEDERAL REPUBLIC OF GERMANY

DO      Donaueschingen, Fürstlich Fürstenbergische Hofbibliothek

HR      Harburg über Donauwörth, Fürstlich Oettingen-Wallerstein'sche Bibliothek und Kunstsammlung, Schloss Harburg (now in Augsburg, Universitätsbibliothek)

Mbs      Munich, Bayerische Staatsbibliothek, Musiksammlung

Rtt      Regensburg, Fürstlich Thurn und Taxis'sche Hofbibliothek

Sl      Stuttgart, Württembergische Landesbibliothek

WD      Wiesentheid, Musiksammlung des Grafen von Schönborn-Wiesentheid

## D-ddr GERMAN DEMOCRATIC REPUBLIC

Ju      Jena, Universitätsbibliothek der Friedrich-Schiller-Universität

RUh      Rudolstadt, Staatsarchiv

SWl      Schwerin, Wissenschaftliche Allgemeinbibliothek

## GB GREAT BRITAIN

Lbm      London, The British Library

## I ITALY

CR      Cremona, Biblioteca statale

Fc      Florence, Biblioteca del Conservatorio di Musica "L. Cherubini"

## NL THE NETHERLANDS

At      Amsterdam, Toonkunst-Bibliotheek

## US UNITED STATES OF AMERICA

BETm      Bethlehem (Pa.), Archives of the Moravian Church in Bethlehem

NYp      New York, Public Library at Lincoln Center

Wc      Washington, DC, Library of Congress, Music Division

*The Symphony 1720–1840*
Barry S. Brook, Editor-in-Chief     Series B-Volume IX-Score 1

# Symphony No. 2 in D major

Them. Index 2

## Friedrich Witt

*Niederstetten 1770–1836 Würzburg*

### Edited by Stephen C. Fisher

p. 3 (3)

p. 51 (51)

p. 79 (79)

p. 90 (90)

**Instrumentation:** 2 violins, viola, bass, flute, 2 oboes, 2 bassoons, 2 horns, 2 trumpets, timpani

**Date:** 1803 or earlier

**Source used for this edition:** Printed parts, Offenbach: André, [*ca.* 1803/1804], "Sinfonie / à / grand orchestre / composée par / F. WITT / Maître de Chapelle à Wurzbourg / No. 2," Washington, DC, Library of Congress, M1001 W835 No. 2p Case

**Editorial remarks:** Editorial additions of accidentals, dynamics, and groups of staccato marks have been bracketed; added slurs and ties are indicated by vertical strokes through them. Inconsistencies in parallel passages have on occasion been altered to bring parts into conformity with one another.

*Garland Publishing, Inc.   New York & London   1983*

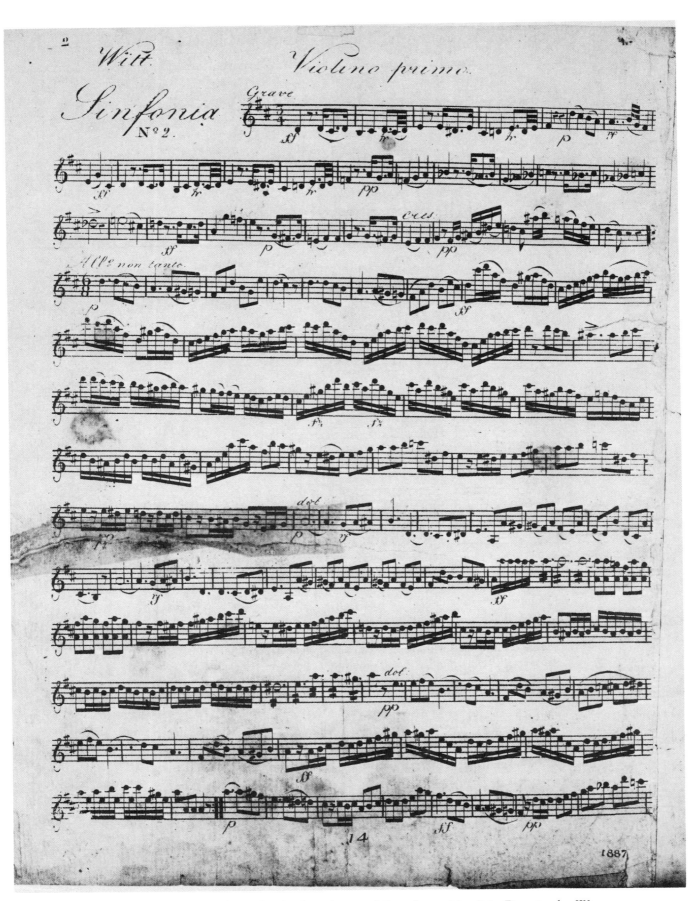

First page of violin I from the André edition of Symphony No. 2 in D major by Witt
(*Washington, Library of Congress*)

# Symphony No. 2 in D major

Edited by Stephen C. Fisher

*Them. Index 2*

Friedrich Witt

20

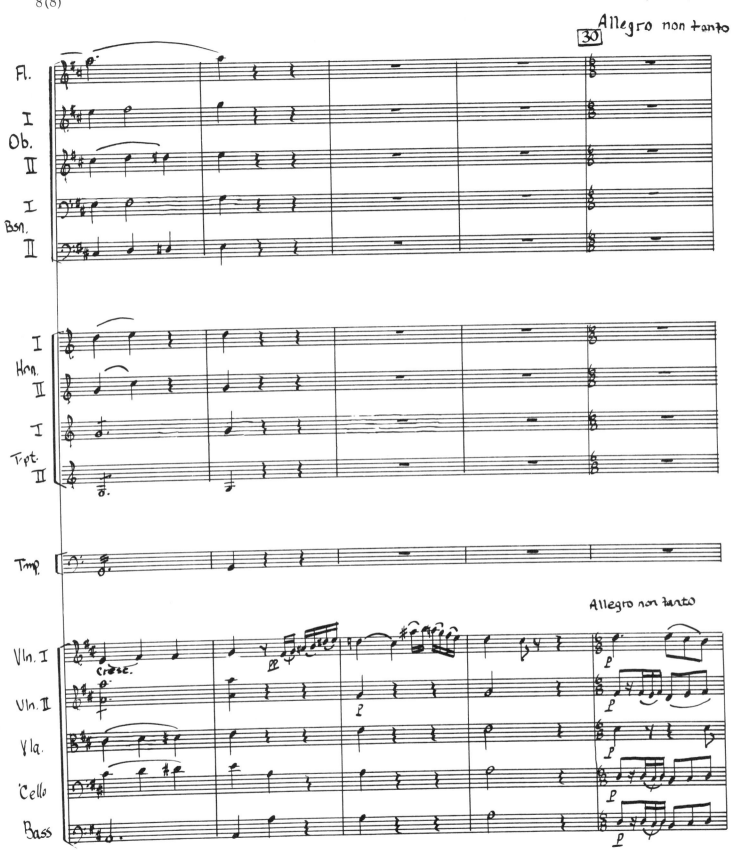

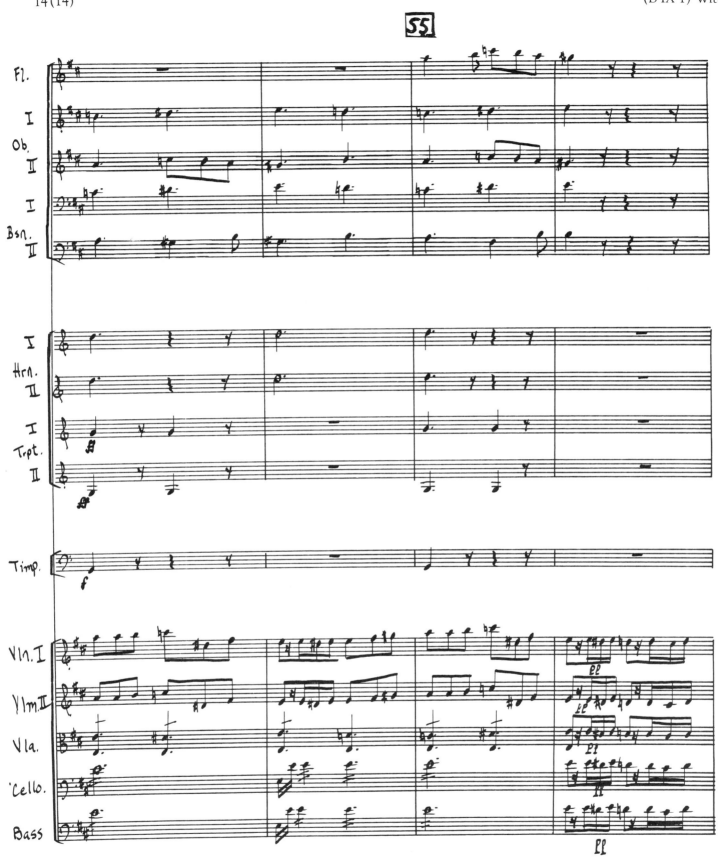

60

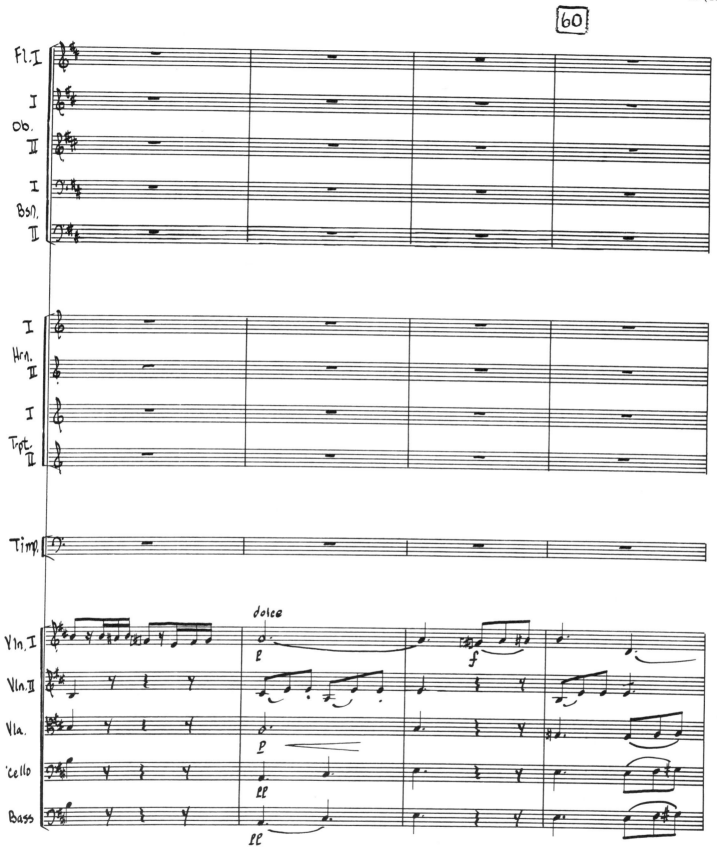

65

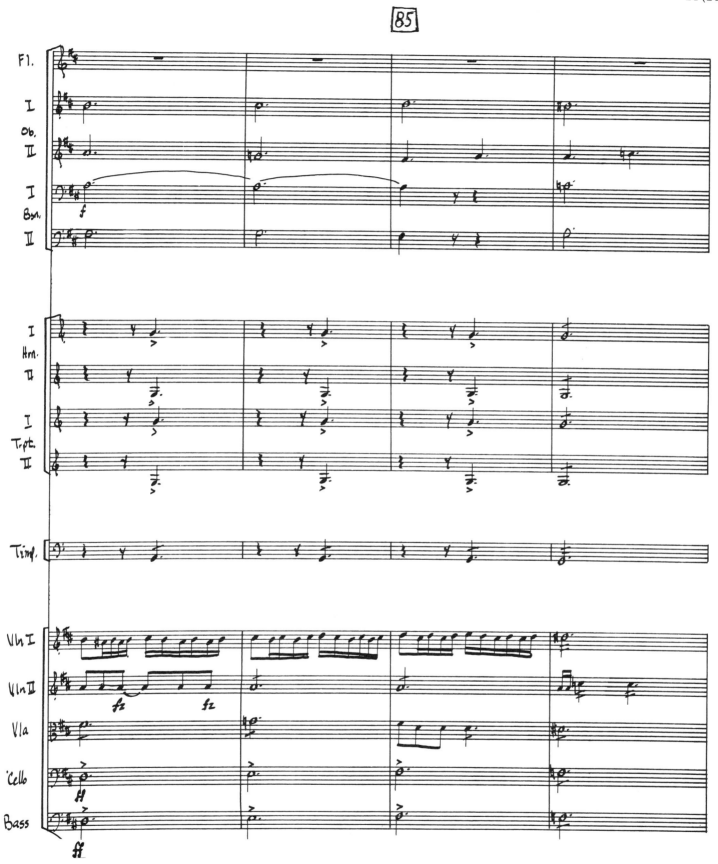

100

110

**120**

125

130

135

140

175
Fl.
I
Ob.
II
I
Bsn.
II
I
Hrn.
II
I
Trpt.
II
Timp.
Vln. I
Vln. II
Vla.
'Cello
Bass
pp
pp
pp

185
Fl.
I
Ob.
II
I
Bsn.
II
pp
pp
I
Hrn.
II
I
Trpt.
II
Timp.
Vln. I
Vln. II
Vla.
Cello
Bass

205

215

220

225

Adagio

II

5

**10**

25
Fl.
Ob.
I
II
Bsn.
I
II
Hrn.
I
II
Vln. I
Vln. II
Vla.
Cello
Bass
tr.
tr.
pp
[pp]

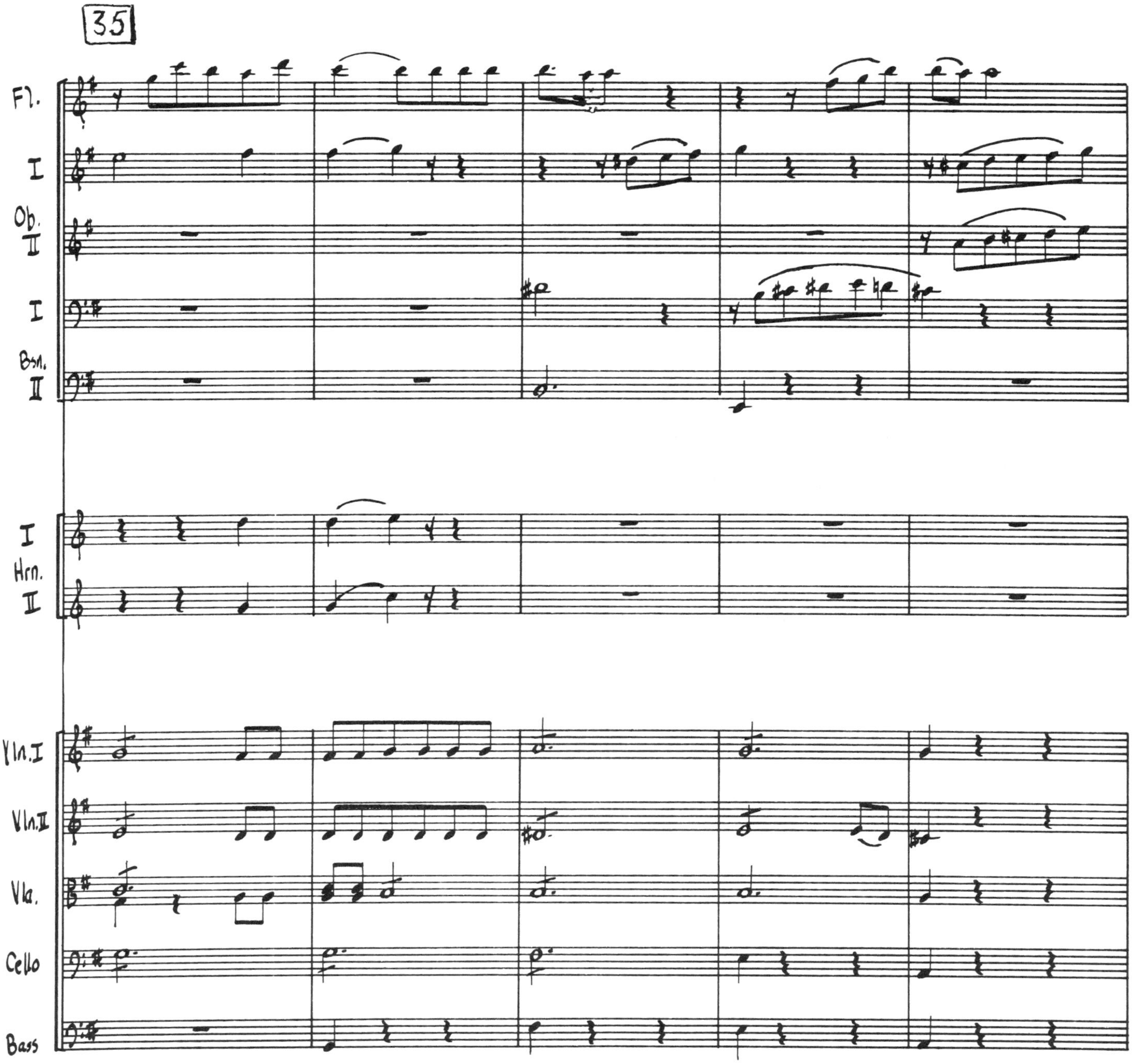
35
Fl.
I
Ob.
II
I
Bsn.
II
I
Hrn.
II
Vln.I
Vln.II
Vla.
Cello
Bass

65
Minore
Fl.
I
Ob.
II
I
Bsn.
II
I
Hrn.
II
Vln. I
Vln. I
Vla.
Cello
Bass
ff
ff
ff
ff
ff

# IV

**Allegro non tanto**

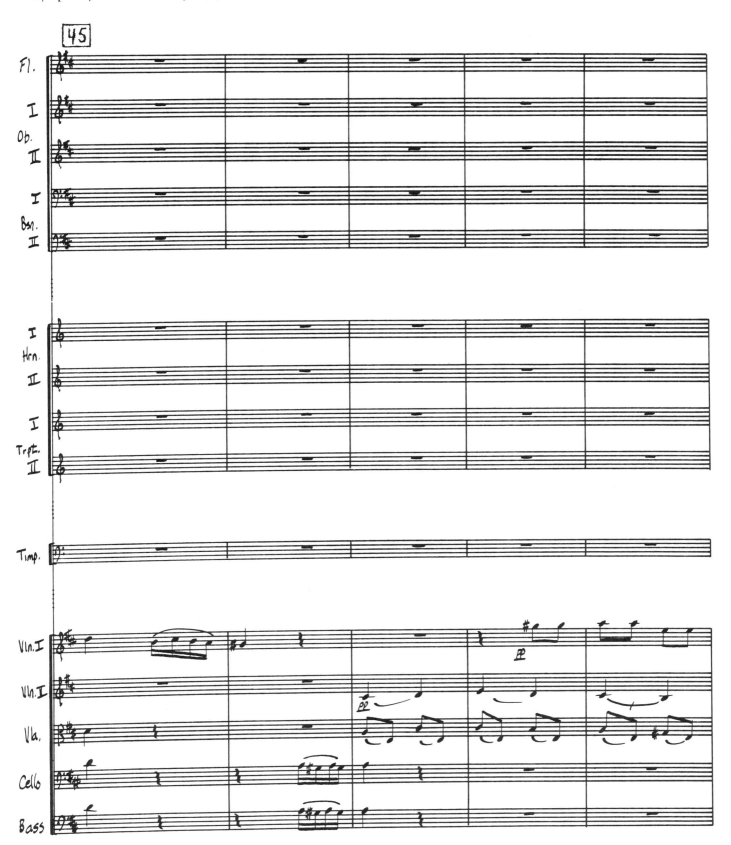

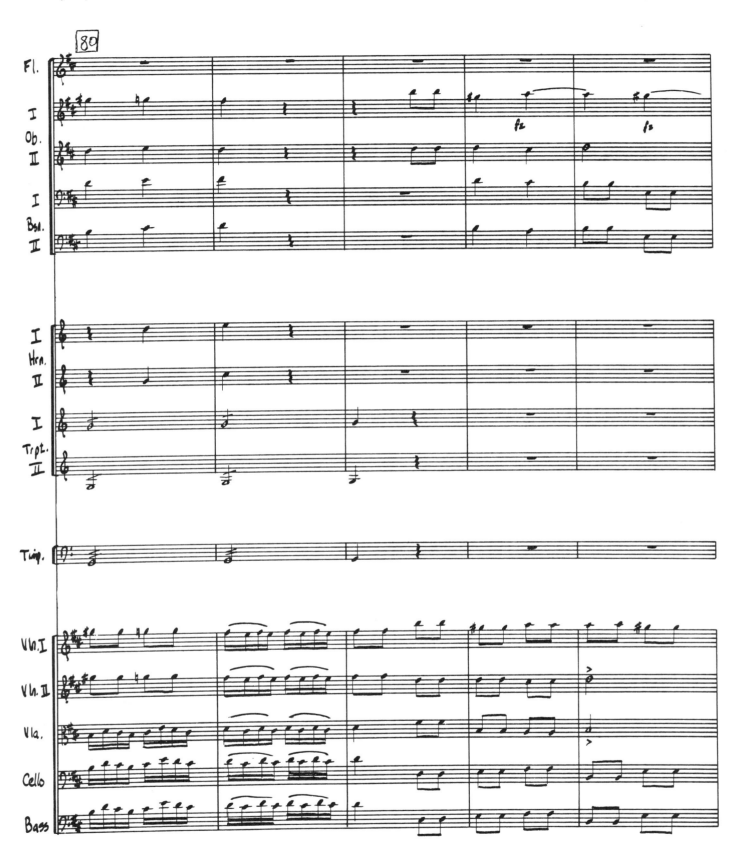

*The Symphony 1720–1840*

Barry S. Brook, Editor-in-Chief    Series B-Volume IX-Score 2

# *Symphonie à petit orchestre* No. 1 in C minor

## Antoine Reicha

*Prague 1770–1836 Paris*

## Edited by Stephen C. Fisher

p. 3 (143)

p. 14 (154)

p. 22 (162)

p. 25 (165)

**Instrumentation:** 2 violins, viola, bass, flute, 2 oboes, 2 bassoons, 2 horns *ad libitum*

**Date:** 1799–1801 or after 1808

**Source used for this edition:** Reicha's autograph, Paris, Bibliothèque nationale, Ms. 14500

**Editorial remarks:** The score has been reproduced from the autograph. Editorial additions have been confined to numbering the measures.

Garland Publishing, Inc.   New York & London   1983

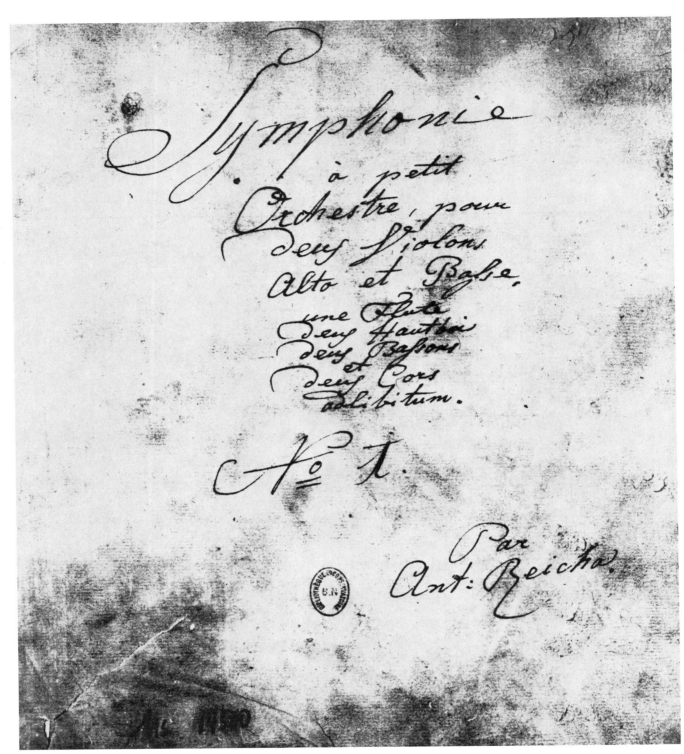

Title page of the autograph manuscript of Reicha's Symphony in C minor
(*Paris, Bibliothèque nationale*)

# Symphonie à petit orchestre No. 1 in C minor

Edited by Stephen C. Fisher

Antoine Reicha

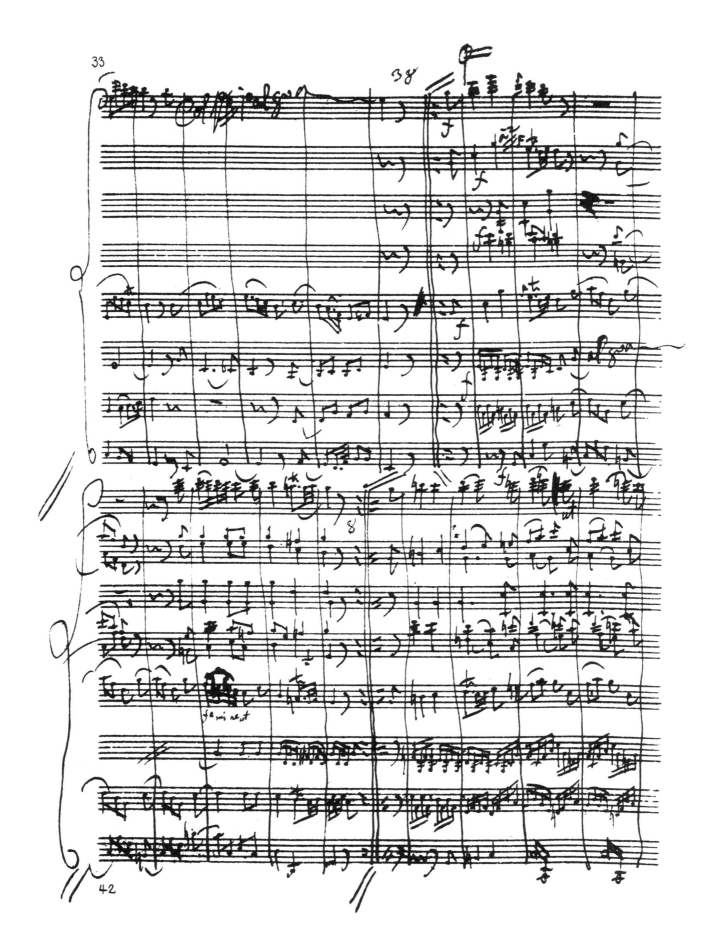

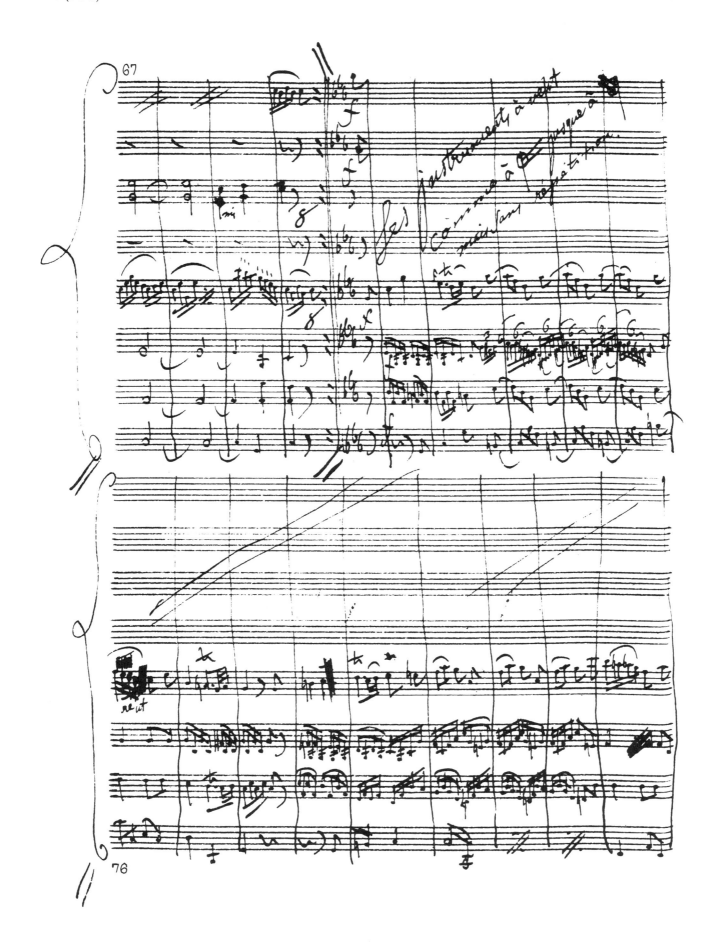

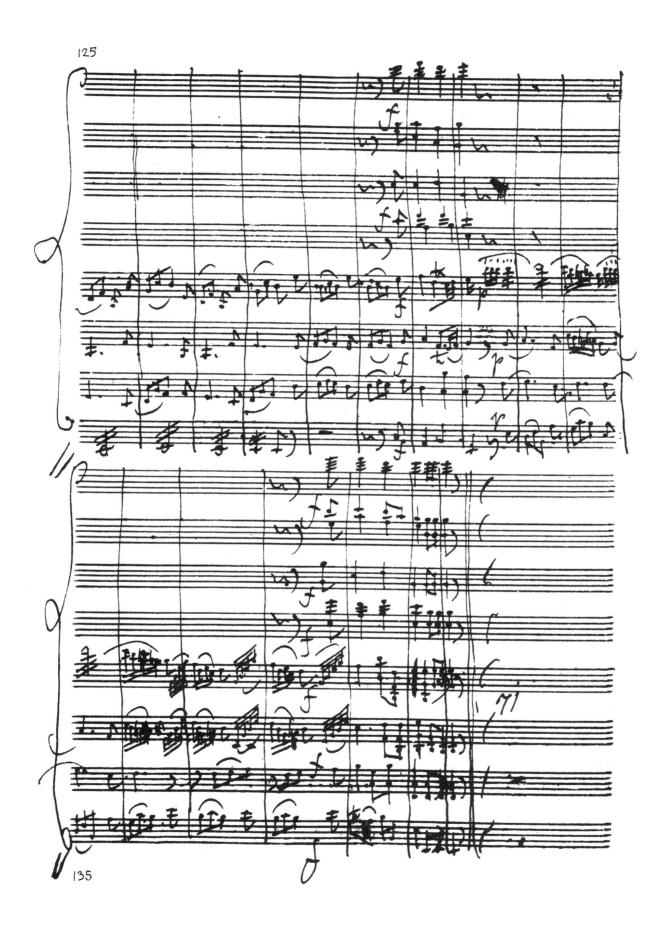

*Menuetto. Alto Vivace.*

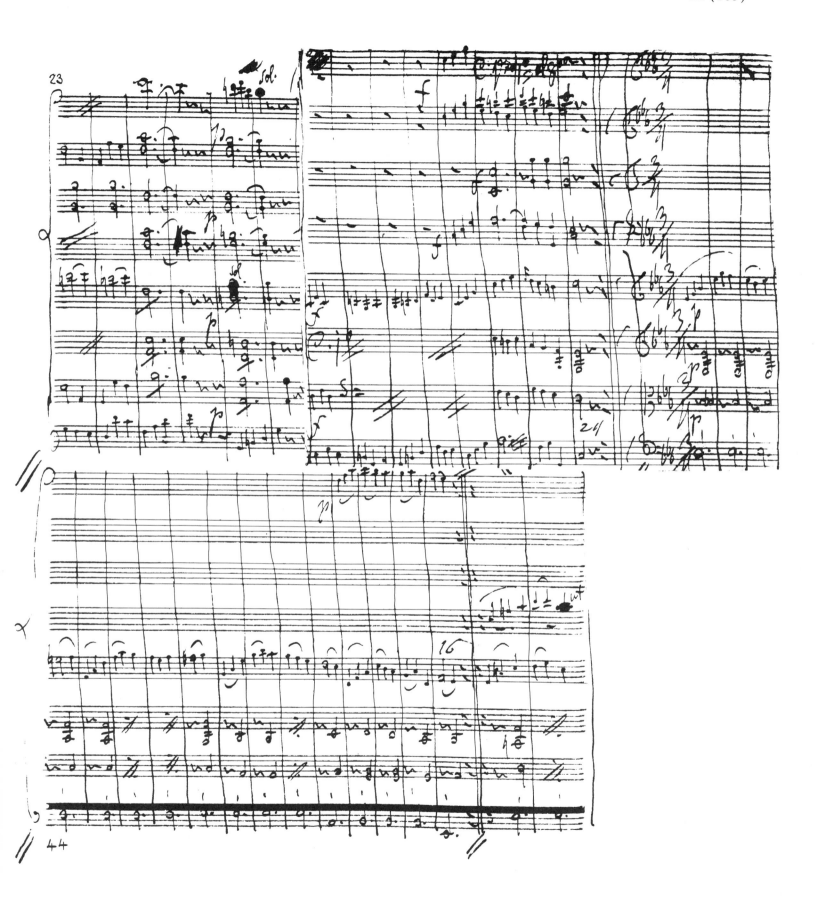

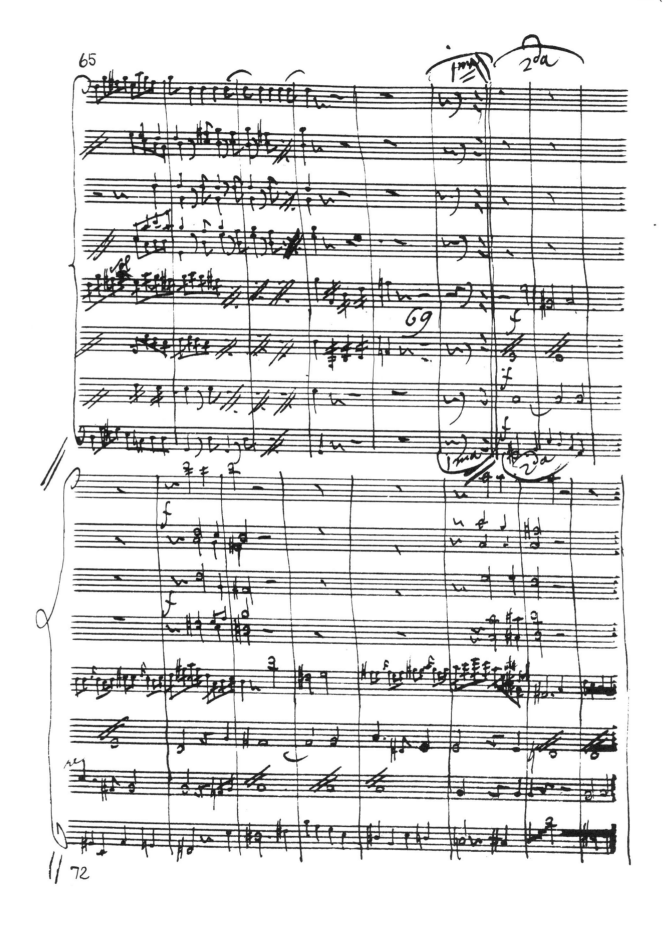

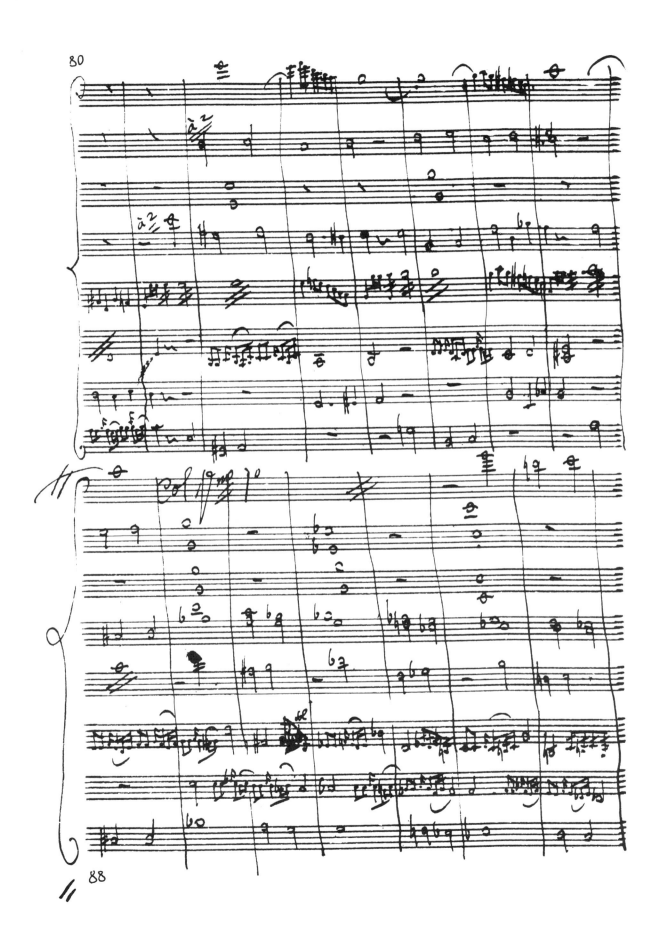

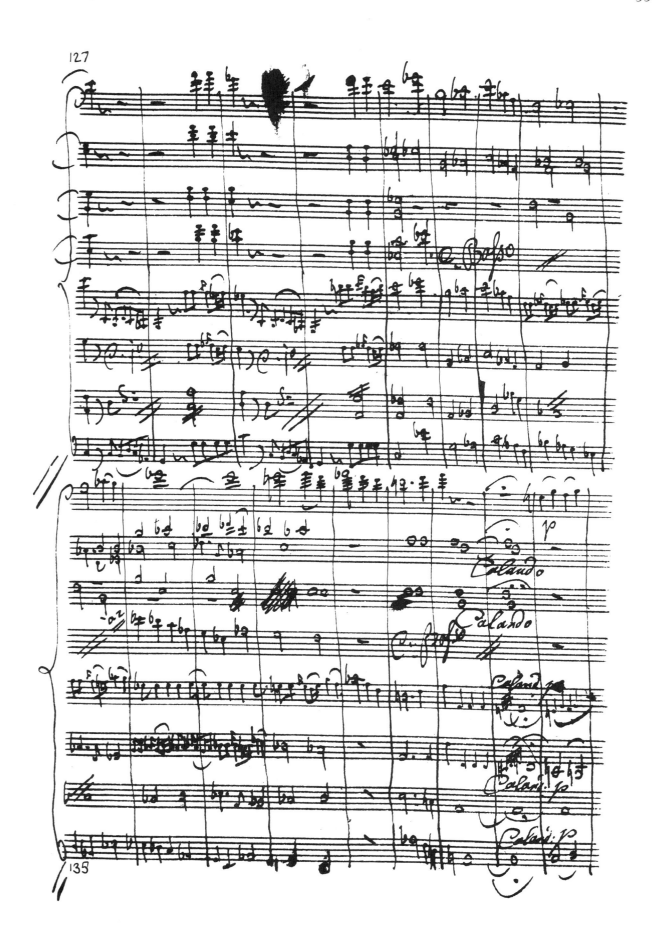

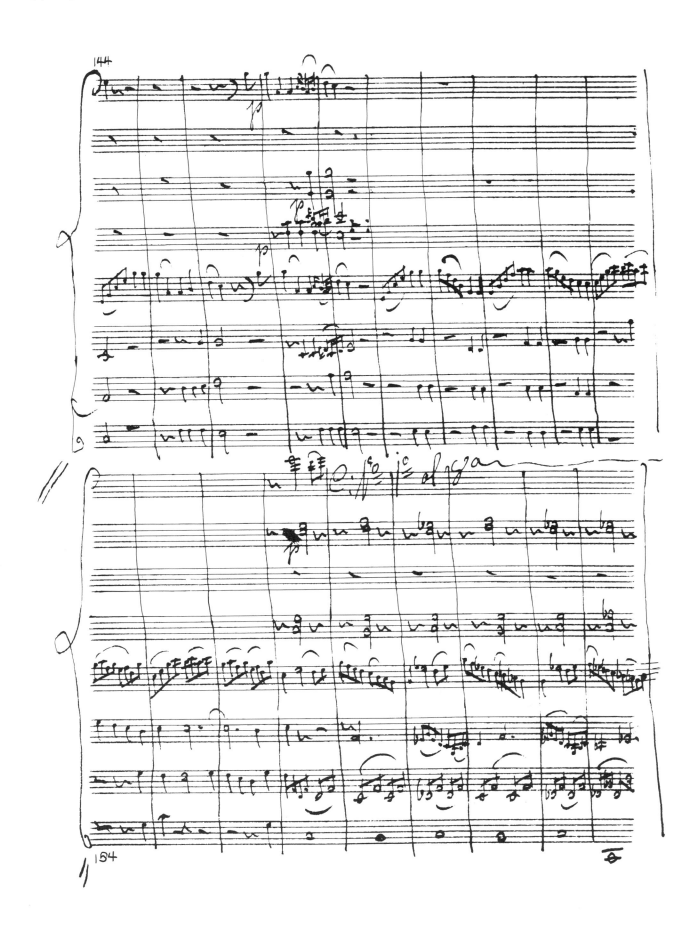

*The Symphony 1720–1840*
Barry S. Brook, Editor-in-Chief    Series B-Volume IX-Score 3

# Symphony No. 3 in F major
## Antoine Reicha
*Prague 1770–1836 Paris*
## Edited by Stephen C. Fisher

p. 3 (179)

p. 23 (199)

p. 33 (209)

p. 42 (218)

**Instrumentation:** 2 violins, viola, bass, flute, 2 oboes, 2 clarinets, 2 bassoons, 2 horns, timpani

**Date:** 4 September 1808; introduction added later

**Source used for this edition:** Reicha's autograph, Paris, Bibliothèque nationale, Ms. 14499

**Editorial remarks:** The main body of the score has been reproduced from the autograph; for reasons of legibility the introduction has been transcribed. Editorial additions have been confined to numbering the measures and adding clarifying comments to Reicha's more extensive revisions.

*Garland Publishing, Inc.*   New York & London   1983

# Symphony No. 3 in F major

Edited by Stephen C. Fisher

Antoine Reicha

235

246

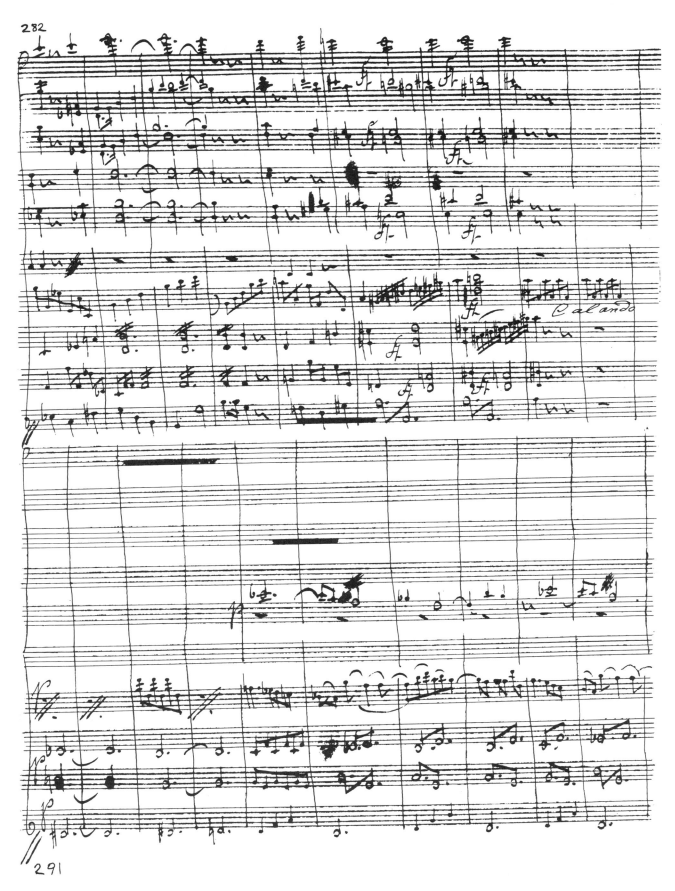

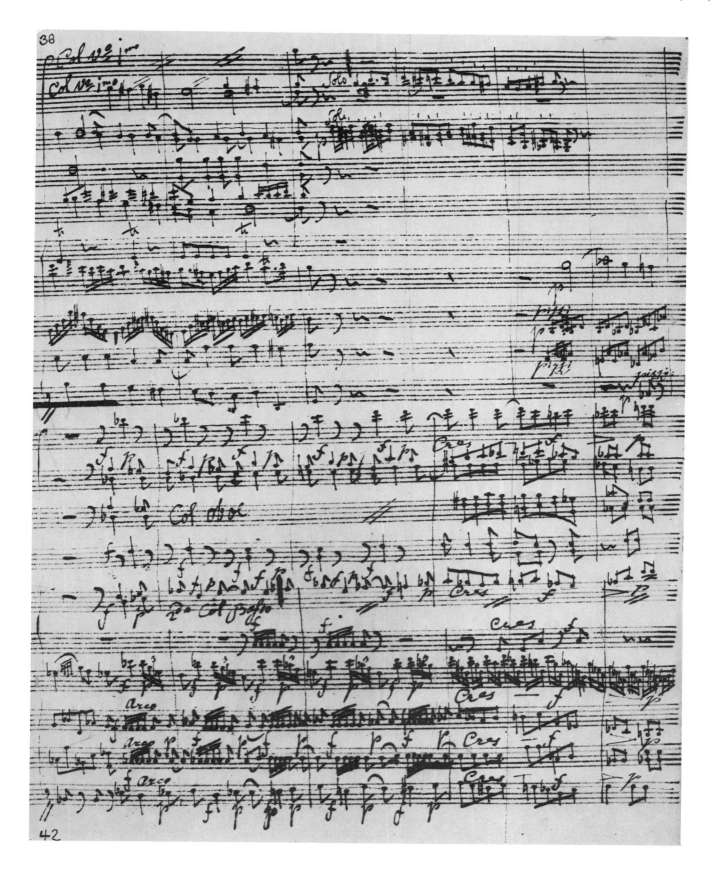

*M. 71A: M. 78–84 follow out of place. M. 84 is the conclusion of the movement. Following m. 78–84 the rest of m. 71 appears (labelled 71B) together with m. 72–77.

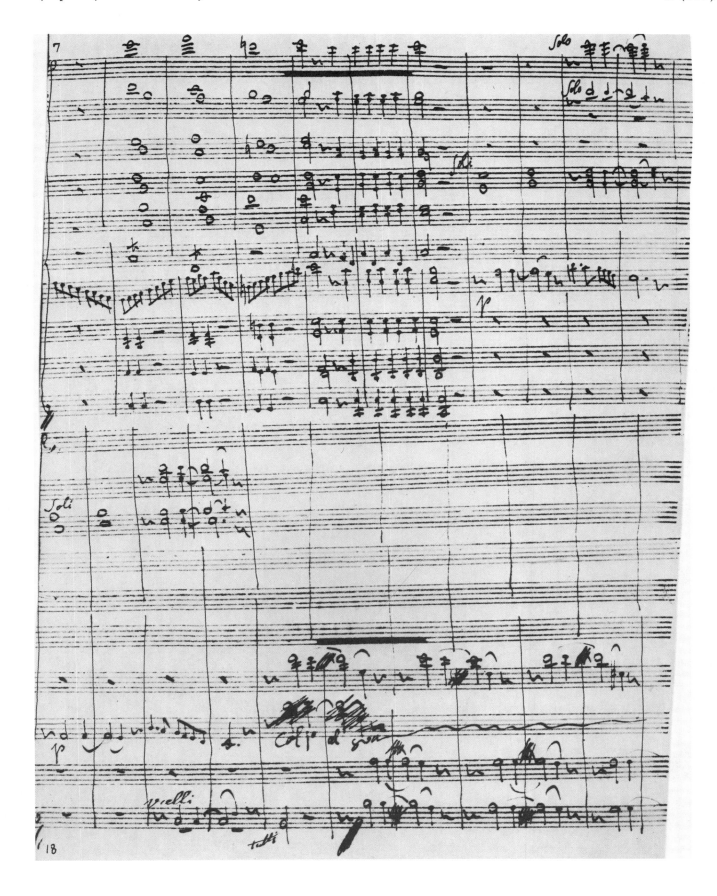

201

210

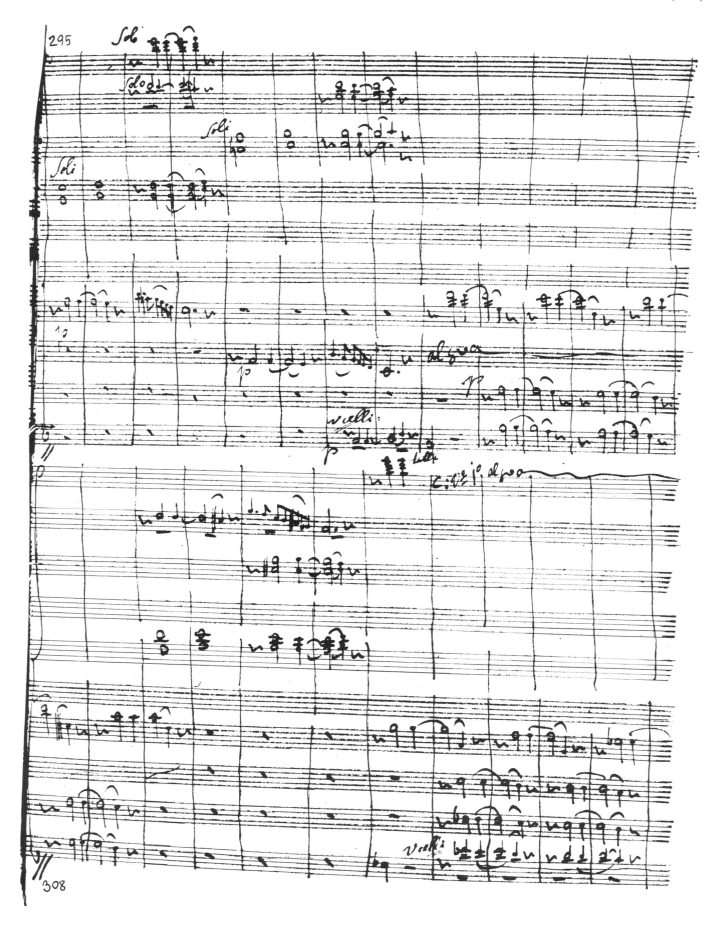

*M. 416: M. 417–18 appear on the last page.

*The Symphony 1720–1840*
Barry S. Brook, Editor-in-Chief    Series B·Volume IX·Score 4

# Symphony in E-flat major, Op. 33
## Anton Eberl
*Vienna 1765–1807 Vienna*
## Edited by Barbara Coeyman and Stephen C. Fisher

Andante sostenuto / Con sord. — Allegro con fuoco e vivace ... p. 3 (245)

Andante con moto ... p. 29 (271)

Menuetto: Allegro vivace ... p. 39 (281)

Finale: Allegro assai ... p. 48 (290)

**Instrumentation:** 2 violins, viola, bass, 2 flutes, 2 oboes, 2 clarinets, 2 bassoons, 2 horns, 2 trumpets, timpani

**Date:** Probably 1803

**Source used for this edition:** Printed parts, Leipzig: Kühnel, [*ca.* 1806], "SIMPHONIE . . . / composée et dediée / à Son Altesse Monseigneur / LE PRINCE REGNANT DE LOBKOWITZ / par / Antoine Eberl./Oe. XXXIII." Washington, Library of Congress, M1001 E16 Op. 33p Case

**Editorial remarks:** Editorial additions of accidentals, dynamics, groups of staccato marks, and notes have been bracketed; added slurs and ties are indicated by vertical strokes through them. Inconsistencies in parallel passages have on occasion been altered to bring parts into conformity with one another.

*Garland Publishing, Inc.    New York & London    1983*

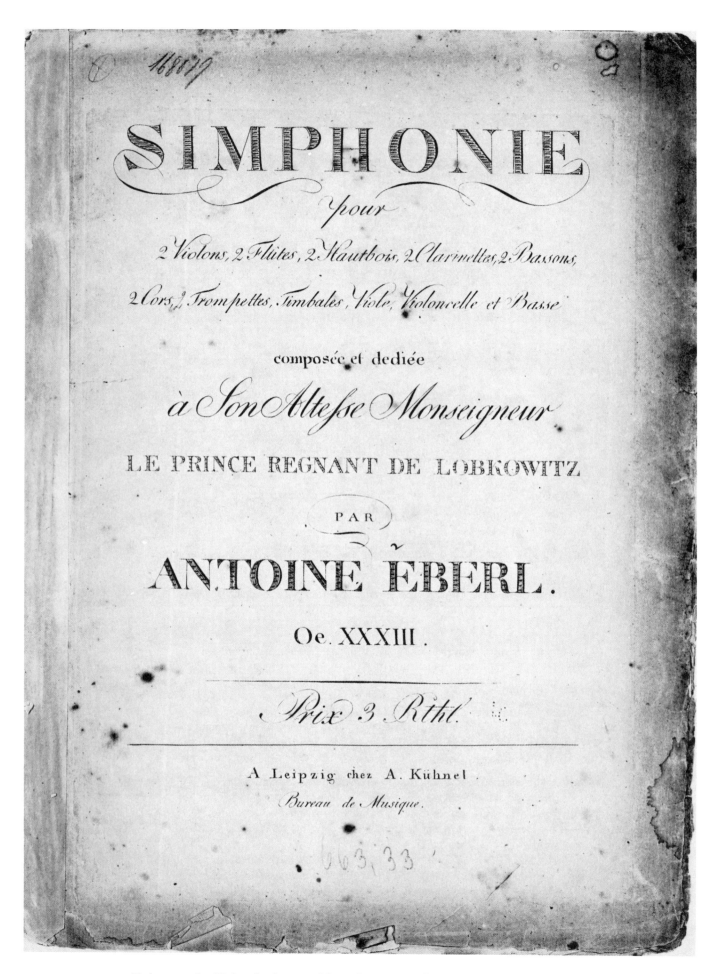

Title page for Kühnel edition of Symphony in E-flat major, Op. 33, by Eberl
(*Washington, Library of Congress*)

# Symphony in E-flat major, Op. 33

Edited by Barbara Coeyman and Stephen C. Fisher

Anton Eberl

Allegro con fuoco e vivace

Vlc e Basso

## II

*M. 51, cl I: ♮ in source

*M. 87, cl II: c#¹ in source

*M. 107, vla: ♭ in source

IV

Finale: Allegro Assai

*M. 133, cor: $c^1/c^2$ in source

*M. 326: Cor have d² in source; b has f in source; cf. m. 104.

*M. 418, cor II: c² in source

# Notes about the Editors

Stephen C. Fisher is currently finishing a doctoral dissertation in the history of music at the University of Pennsylvania on "Haydn's overtures and their use as concert orchestral works." He held a Fulbright-Hays grant in 1976–1977; during research in Europe that year he located the first known complete copies of two Haydn baryton trios that he later edited for inclusion in the *Joseph Haydn Werke*. He has contributed to *Current musicology*, the *Mitteilungen der Internationalen Stiftung Mozarteum*, *Haydn studies: proceedings of the International Haydn Conference, Washington, 1975*, and *Haydn-Studien*. He is editing two volumes of symphonies for the Haydn *Werke* and has additional projects under way concerning Haydn, Eberl, and the Viennese music-copying business in the late eighteenth century.

Barbara Coeyman is a specialist in music of the French Baroque. Her doctoral dissertation in musicology, in progress at the City University of New York, concerns the theatrical works of Michel-Richard Delalande. Her work on it was aided by a Fulbright scholarship to France in 1981–1982. She holds an M.A. in musicology from the University of Pennsylvania. A performer of early music, specializing in Baroque solo and ensemble literature for the bass viol, she has appeared in numerous recitals in Philadelphia, New York, and Pittsburgh. Editorial work has included several editions of viol music and serving as a contributing editor to the Pendragon Press French opera series. She has taught music history and theory at West Chester State College and Brooklyn College and currently teaches viol and coaches early music in Pittsburgh.